DOES MAN HAVE A FUTURE
IN GOD'S UNIVERSE?

"Will the human drama of life on earth be exported to other worlds for endless ages, like special casts taking a hit show on the road, when space travel becomes feasible? Or will it be totally snuffed out as described in Chapter Twenty-four of Saint Matthew, as our little ball of earth goes spiraling back into the sun, from whence it came? Is the earth essentially a grave, a cradle, a test tube, or an incubator?"

Prophetess Jeane Dixon poses this provocative question and—with her special gifts of wisdom and vision—she offers the awesome and inspired answers that have been revealed to her . . .

in
THE CALL TO GLORY

The Call to Glory
JEANE DIXON
Speaks of Jesus

by Jeane Dixon

BANTAM BOOKS · TORONTO · NEW YORK · LONDON
A NATIONAL GENERAL COMPANY

DEDICATED TO MAN
BELIEVING AND UNBELIEVING

—JEANE DIXON

*This low-priced Bantam Book
has been completely reset in a type face
designed for easy reading, and was printed
from new plates. It contains the complete
text of the original hard-cover edition.*
NOT ONE WORD HAS BEEN OMITTED.

THE CALL TO GLORY
*A Bantam Book / published by arrangement with
William Morrow & Company, Inc.*

PRINTING HISTORY
*Morrow edition published 1971
Bantam edition published March 1973*

*Bantam Books are published by Bantam Books, Inc., a National
General company. Its trade-mark, consisting of the words "Bantam
Books" and the portrayal of a bantam, is registered in the United
States Patent Office and in other countries. Marca Registrada.
Bantam Books, Inc., 666 Fifth Avenue, New York, N.Y. 10019.*

PRINTED IN THE UNITED STATES OF AMERICA

Contents

Prologue ... 1

1. Getting to Know Him ... 9
2. The Divine Design ... 20
3. The Prophets and the Promise ... 29
4. "Elijah Is Come Already" ... 37
5. The Call to Glory ... 45
6. The Triple Threat ... 57
7. The Golden Voice of Jesus ... 68
8. What! The Devil?! ... 79
9. The Apostles ... 93
10. Jesus and Women ... 108
11. Living by Faith ... 121
12. The Transfiguration—
    Point of No Return ... 130
13. A Prayer for Judas Iscariot—
    and for Us! ... 140
14. "I Am the Resurrection
    and the Life" ... 150
15. Destiny: The Prophets
    and Our Times ... 160

Epilogue ... 170

With
special
gratitude
to

REVEREND
STEPHEN HARTDEGEN,
O.F.M.,
my personal religious consultant
for this book

and

With sincere appreciation to
Reverend *STEPHEN BREEN, Ph.D.*
LAWRENCE SOMMERS
WILLIAM H. GRAHAM
for their scholarly help and friendly
encouragement

"Things that are impossible for men are possible for God." (Luke 18:27.)

With God's help, all things are possible to man.
—Jeane Dixon

Prologue

As we draw nearer to the end of the twentieth century, we see that it is not any single dilemma that confronts us, but a bewildering array of chaotic conditions, brought about by man himself because of his selfish greed for money and power. We are faced with unrest and upheaval in every area of our lives, our nation, and in every corner of the globe. Clearly, we need to know who we are, our purpose in living, and how our lives fit together in the overall plan of God.

If we are surrounded by darkness, we must grope for a light.

Our situation today seems to be one of complete bewilderment. Many questions regarding these chaotic conditions find expression in the poet Wordsworth's query:

> Whither is fled the visionary gleam?
> Where is it now, the glory and the dream?

Let me remind you that the glory and the dream have NOT fled. Nor can they, because the glory and the dream are God's divine plan for all of us. We must have the vision to look beyond the chaos and believe that revolution is evolution in process. This is what faith is for—to believe—to believe and know that we are created

1

with an individual talent for a specific mission, fulfilling our purpose at the precise right time in the history of man, progressing in the upward spiral of human development—ever onward to higher spiritual understanding.

Our human plans are not always in accord with God's plan. God alone is great enough to bring good out of what appears to us to be tragic, evil, and even hopeless at times. With the certain knowledge that God has given us the light to find our way out of the darkness, we can look at the situation with the assurance that through faith and work all obscurity will be overcome.

However much we may wish to look backward with fondness to the comfortable values and feelings of security associated with the past, we must not do so. We must learn from the past—not live in the past. We must live in the present, with an eye on the future. It is what we do each day—our thoughts, words, and deeds—that determines what the future will be.

We are in the process of constructing a new world—a world in accordance with God's plan, His plan for all of us upon this earth. The many revolutions going on in America and throughout the world now seem necessary to call attention to neglected human needs. But there may come a time when revolution in itself is self-defeating.

There must be food, clothing, shelter, education, transportation, business, and government of one sort or another. We cannot all surf endlessly in Florida, California, or Hawaii! Even if we could, there would still be work to be done and responsibilities in society to be met by someone. It is teamwork we need; teamwork and understanding. Regardless of the political climate, whether it be liberal, conservative, or radical, each one must share responsibility.

So, even though we go on dismantling our religion, discrediting our faith, demeaning our leadership, dumping radioactive wastes into the ocean, banking nuclear fire in underground silos, befouling our environment, squandering our resources, demoralizing our citizens, throwing away our culture, wasting our talents, worshiping the power of the almighty dollar, mistaking the trees for the forest, and a thousand other stupidities—we shall overcome! The last quarter of this century will prepare us for the greater and better life beginning with the new century after 2000 A.D.

But it will not be easy! I have likened the pilgrimage of humanity during the remainder of our century to Socrates in prison, to Christ in Gethsemane. I have not chosen my words idly. There are dark days ahead. The age of nationalism, a corruption of religion, is nearly over. A new era of universalism is close at hand. Its religious inspiration will be centered in Israel. We are on the brink of changes, in both church and state, which will go to the roots of civilization.

I often make the observation in my lectures that the life of the golden age of great empires is usually two hundred years, and this pattern has prevailed throughout history. A people go from bondage to faith, from faith to courage, from courage to liberty, from liberty to abundance, from abundance to selfishness, from selfishness to complacency, from complacency to apathy, from apathy to dependence, and from dependence back into bondage; nine crucial stages in the rise, decline, and fall of empires.

We are now approaching our two hundredth anniversary as a nation. Are our people abdicating their personal liberties and slipping into a state of complete dependency—the last stage prior to the return of bondage? Are we turning over our rights and responsibilities piecemeal to agencies of government? Are we forsaking the values that made us great, those of the founding fathers, crystallized in the motto: In God We Trust? I ask you to think well and draw your own conclusions.

The "American experiment" is capable of greater

promise than it has yet achieved. It need not follow the mother country and its other component cultures into decrepitude and decay after only two hundred years. There is a great and beautiful potential here, waiting only for unification of our people.

My own solution to the problem is an ancient and reliable one—religion. Religion, as Dr. Toynbee says, is the medium that bears life through a dark age, from the crumbling of one culture to the birth of another age.

This is the time when religion is doubly essential to utilize the greatness and understanding of human beings and to open our whole world to the realization and fulfillment of our potential. These goals cannot be accomplished by leadership alone, however great. We cannot continue to be divided; we must unite as one people, not only under God but under our government as well, as *one nation*.

Is this so difficult? No, it need not be—not if we seek inspiration. It is for that very reason I propose the Prince of Peace as the source of our inspiration.

From the time Jesus was born in Bethlehem He has made an extraordinary impact on history. He never killed anyone, never hurt anyone, never made a fortune, had no modern inventions or comforts, never wrote a book, never in all His journeys traveled over a hundred miles from His birthplace. But, as Father Teilhard de Chardin wrote, "the figure of Christ (not only as described in a book but as realized in the concrete in Christian consciousness) is so far the most perfect approximation to a final and total object toward which the universal human effort can tend without becoming wearied or deformed." (*Building the Earth*, Teilhard de Chardin. Wilkes-Barre, Pa: Dimension Books, p. 40.)

It surprises no one to hear Jesus cited as the most perfect man who ever lived. Christian faith and dynamism at their best have been inspired by this ideal. Even today it is taking root and spreading in the lives of many American youths partly as a result of their unprecedented experience with LSD, marijuana, and heroin. Our precious youth, having run the full gamut of rejection in all directions, now have begun to accept the truth in their return to Jesus and His teachings.

Jesus was indeed an instrument of God. The transformation He worked in His original followers, from frightened innovators to creative leaders, is the same one we need now on a scale appropriate to the space age.

Western civilization has been built on the Judeo-Christian tradition for many centuries. Only twice have there been serious attempts to do away with this religion as such: during the Reign of Terror following the French Revolution, when supposed reason officially replaced faith; and under the Soviets in modern Russia, who have tried to do the same thing. The Reign of Terror was well named. It was a period of bloody chaos which ended only with the restoration of religion as a part of society. In Russia and her satellites, after decades of communism, while some well-being exists, it exists in a profound spiritual void under a reign of terror. But there is still a wellspring of religion left. As the citizens of those countries learned to their sorrow, when people lose their religion, their loss of humanity and dignity is not far behind. The day will come when they will be converted.

There can be no doubt of the signs of our times. Already, the destruction of our religious heritage has begun with appalling consequences: drug abuse, alcoholism, the breakdown of law and public administration, the rising tide of violence, and the deterioration of family life. The only antidote to these evils is to stand firm in our faith and withstand all attempts to drive God from our lives. "Go, therefore, and make disciples of all the nations," said Jesus, and those of us who believe must labor to fulfill His command (Matthew 28:19).

It has been said that anyone attempting to write

about Jesus of Nazareth tells more about himself than about Jesus. So be it! Those acquainted with my life know that God's presence has been as familiar to me as it was to Abraham and Moses, that like Mary Magdalene on Easter morning I have looked into the face of the risen Jesus and heard His voice. These experiences are not as extraordinary as they may at first appear; they have happened to many. To find God through Jesus one need only seek with serious dedication and perseverance—and that is the meaning of prayer. We need to pray with the simplicity of childlike faith: "Ask and you shall receive, seek and you shall find, knock and it shall be opened to you." For, "The heavenly Father will give the Holy Spirit to those who seek Him." (Luke 11:9, 13.)

From Cardinal Ottaviani to Harvey Cox of Harvard, men of religion are reexamining the history of theology and Scripture for a new spiritual center of gravity. When Champollion found the Rosetta stone in Egypt, when Schliemann began to dig at Troy and Sir Arthur Evans in Crete, they were digging to get, if possible, to the bottom of things; they were like shock troops in search for some understanding of the historical Jesus. Despite the wealth of material accumulated down through the centuries on the subject of the central character of Western history, Jesus, there is hardly a shred of information outside of the Gospels documenting the most significant life ever lived! Incredible as it seems, Pontius Pilate kept no records (that we know of) and wrote no relevant letters. Neither did Annas, Caiaphas, Gamaliel, or anyone else. The Dead Sea Scrolls are seemingly mute. Tacitus, Josephus, Suetonius came along too late. Only the little fragment attributed to Publius Lentulus, describing Jesus as a "prophet of great truth," floats like a telltale bit of wreckage on the surface of that crucial, contemporary history. Only the misty "Shroud of Turin," the cloth in which the body of Jesus was wrapped, pretends to be an actual likeness. In purely historic annals, the life of Jesus passed almost unnoticed! And therefore one turns exclusively to the four Gospels.

We know that Saint John, the "beloved disciple," lived to the end of the first century. The writing of his gospel came later than the other three. It is not so much a narration as a theologian's exposition of Jesus as the great redeemer. Luke, the Greek physician, arrived late on the scene and had no contact with Jesus, relying on the other apostles for his literary testament. The remaining two, Matthew and Mark, were eyewitnesses of many of the events they narrate. One reads them all, like the accounts of four adventurers sharing a common experience, and gradually into one's consciousness there filters a basic awareness of how it really was.

Was Jesus of Nazareth truly divine? This question is still asked. Yet Jesus expressly said so when addressing Himself to His fellow Jews on the Feast of the Dedication of the Temple: "The Father and I are one." To show that His listeners understood His answer in the sense of equality with God, we read that the Jews replied: "You who are only a man are making yourself God." (John 10:30-33.)

When Philip said to Jesus during His last discourse to the apostles: "Lord . . . show us the Father and that will be enough for us," "Philip," Jesus replied . . . "Whoever has seen me has seen the Father." (John 14:8-9.)

My own creed is simple: Yes, Jesus was divine as well as human with His two distinct natures united in the single divine Person. In the language of classic theology He is one with the Father and the Holy Spirit, the Son of God who became man of the Holy Spirit, and was born of the Virgin Mary.

In writing of the humanity of the boy Jesus at the age of twelve, Saint Luke states, "Jesus, for his part, progressed steadily in wisdom and age and grace before God and men." (Luke 2:52.) Jesus as man grew to know who

He was and that He could call Himself in truth both "Son of God" and "Son of Man." He was the Son of God, and as man He accepted His role as Messiah.

There was no confusion in this union of the human with the divine in the person of Christ. The miracles He wrought were manifestations of divine power, yet He used His human body and its senses to perform them. As man He is born an infant, grows, develops in mind and body. As God He rises from the tomb on the third day after death.

Not only His life and death, but even more, His Resurrection, established Jesus of Nazareth as truly divine. The stories that have followed His life on earth for twenty centuries have amply vindicated any claims to His unique status in the great scheme of things. History is His real vindicator, the witness of two millennia. To the ends of the earth those who knew and revered Him have carried His message of Love and Goodwill toward men, the essence of God's plan. It is still the best blueprint for our lives in a groping world.

This book is my humble effort, as one Christian, to restate that blueprint in our time.

"Come to terms with him to be at peace. In this shall good come to you." (Job 22:21.)

Our acceptance of and action upon divine guidance is the only way to spiritual harmony, contentment, happiness, and prosperity . . .

—Jeane Dixon

1. Getting to Know Him

Getting to know Jesus Christ is *THE* answer for today's way of life; His life and teachings are blueprints for a groping world. A truth has been spoken: that Jesus Christ IS; that He is active and the central fountain of our life, love, and wisdom today as truly as He ever was or ever will be. In Jesus Christ, God Himself took human form so that we human beings could understand and know Him better. Let us acquaint ourselves with that event which revolutionized the religion of man—the first Christmas.

Did you ever stop to think how few people are born in a stable? No need to say reservations were unnecessary, and, not to sound sacrilegious, a stable has never been the ideal place for childbirth! Let us just say this was God's simple way of beginning a whole new era. By bringing His only Son into the world in a stable He emphasized once and for all the importance of Christ's life and death.

Surely the Prince of Peace did not need to begin His "reign" on earth with glamour, social position, and material wealth.

In turn, Jesus emphasized by the way He lived and taught that His kingdom was of the spirit—the Spirit that is the source of all human energy and achievement— rather than of worldly pomp and power.

Jesus of Nazareth began life as a fugitive. At the height of His mission of salvation He was reviled, persecuted, ridiculed, scourged, cursed, and spat upon and deserted. People called Him impostor, liar, devil, fraud, and fool. The more He pursued His mission of spreading the Word of God, the more certain it became that He would have to fight and die for it. Furthermore, His entire life was one of contradiction. Its climax is found in His death by crucifixion and His Resurrection, which forever disproves the power of death. What a legacy He left mankind!

Yet the child Jesus is "unknown" in the pages of history. Records of children were not kept as they are today. Cameras and family albums were unknown. Mary and Joseph undoubtedly talked much of their Son, as all parents do, but did not record the facts of His growing and learning or humorous sayings and incidents, but we can be sure He was active—eager to find out and discover all of life that flashed before Him. Incidents such as His Shema School training wherein the faith and the history of His people were taught left a record that He was able to speak with authority of the Scripture, of the Law and the Prophets. When He was twelve years of age and went up with Mary and Joseph to Jerusalem, He reportedly wandered from them, causing them great anxiety as they searched for Him. Actually He remained in the temple while the other youths went to enjoy the festivities of the joyous event. When His mother and foster father finally discovered Him in the temple, exchanging knowledge with the scribes and teachers of the Law, Mary and Joseph's anxious pleas as to why Jesus had caused them such fear and concern were answered by Him with love: "Why did you search for me? Did you not know I had to be in my Father's house?" (Luke 2:49.) Jesus' awareness of who He was and what His mission was to be is clearly shown to us in this scriptural passage. He had to accomplish His Father's will.

As a youth growing to manhood we can well imagine that Jesus did not spend His time idly sitting about the streets, passing the time of day. As His awareness increased, so did His thirst for knowledge. He did not spend His time in one place. Imagine yourself as a teen-ager; today's phases and passing fancies are not solely of this age; they are cycles of every age. Jesus Himself was a hardy, robust person, so we can imagine His taking advantage of every opportunity available to Him. This included talk fests with men in the streets, even journeying to areas not in His immediate vicinity.

We can see this wandering youth joyously going about, discovering the teachings and beliefs of His day. Recently ancient scrolls have been brought to light in the area of the Dead Sea, which tell of the strict manner of life and of the study and copying of the Scriptures practiced by a sect called the Essenes. They were dedicated to the preservation of religious beliefs and practices. It is possible that both Jesus and John, the Baptizer, knew the Essenes and may even have visited them, though the Gospel makes no mention of them.

Wherever Jesus went and whatever Jesus did, He had been given a firm background in what had been known, taught, and prophesied in His time. Jesus was indeed more than a mere man. He was filled with divine wisdom and love and He began His mission of humanitarianism, revealing His Father as a God of love and spreading what even to this day is primarily simple: if you really love your God you will instantly love one another as He did and proved by His great sacrifice for others.

As to what happened to separate John from Jesus we are not certain. Perhaps John had learned what knowledge was necessary for him to begin his baptism of repentance and then took off ahead of Jesus as if he were the organizer. Jesus was thirty years of age when He saw John again baptizing and preparing the way for the Messiah foretold by the prophet Malachi: "Lo, I am sending my messenger to prepare the way before me; and suddenly there will come to the temple the Lord whom you seek, and the messenger of the covenant whom you desire. Yes, he is coming, says the Lord of hosts. But who will endure the day of his coming? And who can stand when he appears?" (Malachi 3:1-2.) Although mankind should have been ready for the coming of the Lord and His messenger, the prophet denies that his people will be ready.

We can even say that *mankind* was not yet ready, even as today we do not appear to be ready or maybe not willing to understand God's will. God's plans are sometimes slowed down because man, through his free will and by choice, detours from them. Remember that your Creator made you with freedom of choice. You cannot alter permanently what is divinely preordained, but by your freedom of choice you can alter the divine timetable. And remember, we do not always know to what end the plan is leading. Faith, the bedrock conviction that I often speak of, is not only necessary, it is the very essence that will be useful to God in bringing about on schedule what He wants for us. His timing is not governed by hours, or days, or even years, as we know them.

As an example, let us use an event that happened after one certain Crucifixion! Have you ever wondered about the strange difficulty the apostles and disciples of Jesus Christ had in recognizing Him after the Resurrection? Ask yourself if you were one of the disciples what would you have done upon the death of one whom you had so revered? You had been told that you were to see Him; you loved Him more than you could put into words; but when He died, all you wanted to believe, had actually begun to accept, had completely evaporated! You had no proof that what had been said would come about. You needed something tangible. You needed proof.

Does it seem likely that the confusion of the apostles was the result of their being startled upon perceiving marked alterations in the appearance of the body of Jesus, a ghostlike form, perhaps? This was certainly not intended by the writers of the Scriptures! There was far more than mere symbolism in His difference of appearance.

The changed appearance of Jesus, the Christ, was meant to establish clearly in the disciples' minds the "new creature," the ability to alter appearance and yet always remain the same.

A crucifixion did not destroy Jesus Christ because He rose again. And through His Resurrection He was placed in the now of today, tomorrow, and forever. Jesus told His beloved disciples before leaving this world to return to His Father that He would nevertheless be with them always, until the end of the world (Matthew 28:20). He is indeed present in and through His churches and our hearts to all men and at all times. Jesus, identifying Himself with those who believed in Him, says to Saul, the persecutor of His disciples, "Saul, Saul, why do you persecute me?" indicating thereby that He lived on in His disciples and they in Him (Acts 9:4). He will be seen where people least expect to find him.

The appearance of Jesus, then, was to be a manifestation of humanity as He might least likely be expected to look. For example, you might have shaken hands with Him and not have known whose hand you were shaking, except that the hand may have been unusually warm, not physically so but perceived that way by a penetrating, tingling sensation. Maybe the eyes were unusual; not in color, although they were brilliantly clear and sparkling, but with a depth of love and serenity that cannot be described in words.

The sudden appearances of Jesus in a room where the apostles assembled were intended to show that Jesus was, and indeed is, present, permanently present, and able to show Himself at any time. I have seen Him. Many have; I am sure that these personal and overwhelmingly "nearer to thee" experiences are as unique as the persons themselves. To find God the Father through Jesus one need only seek seriously with dedication and perseverance. That, my friends, is prayerful, childlike expectancy. That is the meaning of prayer, so one can pray with simplicity. "Ask and you shall receive," for "the heavenly Father will give the Holy Spirit to those who ask Him." (Luke 11:9, 13.) In fact, I am sure there are those today who have seen and felt the presence of the Christ and did not know it for what it truly was. But the importance of Christ's appearances or manifestations at any time is that He is thus giving a visible indication of a real but invisible Presence; for "Where two or three are gathered in my name, there am I in their midst." (Matthew 18:20.)

So how can we know Jesus, the Christ? This is the same man who was baptized at the age of thirty in the River Jordan. Jesus primarily taught love: love of God, love of neighbor, and love of self. For true love of God gives us true love of self—without which we lose dignity, self respect, and self-confidence.

These are different aspects of the all-embracing dynamic creation you can be. We are helping to build eternity now. Jesus taught this two thousand years ago and continues to teach and demonstrate it now and always in and through each one of us.

God's creation is His kingdom. Part of this kingdom is on earth and we are therefore a very important part of it; that kingdom is *the here* and *the now*. Jesus Himself is part of that kingdom He preached. His major message was if we follow His teachings and strive for the kingdom of God while on earth, then we will have a much better life on this earth, and the assurance of eternal life in heaven.

This kingdom was first manifested in love and good

works: He taught that the kingdom of God was already among the people to whom He preached by reason of His presence. Where Jesus is, there the kingdom of God is. The kingdom of God is like the treasure hidden in a field, which a man found and covered up; then in his joy he sold all that he had and bought that field (Matthew 13:44). The kingdom of God is already within you if God dwells in you.

The most fascinating part of the story of Jesus is that it gives us eternal hope. Every contact with Jesus reveals some new subtlety or insight about the nature of God as it is reflected in man, and the heights of achievement that are potential in every one of us. Meditation and deep study can bring out the full significance of His life and teachings for everyone's individual life. Reading the factual data nourishes our intellect. Going one step further from the intellectual to the spiritual part we can emotionally share His experiences. Here we go from the reasoning intellect to the intuitive instinct of spirit. Then we find great joy; joy in which one relinquishes self to the spirit and man realizes that knowledge has been given him. For such is God's grace.

I believe some aspects of the life and teachings of Jesus have been hidden until now, and the focus of our age points them up in ways that only the advancement of science and the progress of human thought and intuition can bring forth. I believe these insights into spiritual reality merit our attention, for neglecting them imperils humanity.

The Divine Son of Almighty God, Jesus, the Christ, did not just happen. His coming into the world was foreordained, prophesied, and prepared for. All human history, before and since, bears the impression of Jesus the Christ. The historical being Jesus was born through a Divine Plan, the Master Plan of God. The present Jesus Christ becomes known by bringing the knowledge of His historical life and teachings into our own lives;

this is the way we bring Jesus Christ into our own lives, for was it not He who said, "I am the way, and the truth, and the life" (John 14:6).

What did Jesus actually do?

There is no need to theorize about the life and teaching of Jesus. That record is immortalized in the four Gospels.

What is the significance of all these records? Jesus knew who He was and what His purpose and mission were.

When John and Jesus met at the River Jordan it was more than a meeting of two mere men. The River Jordan meeting began the teaching ministry of Jesus as had been previously foretold, and it was there that John had been preparing for Jesus' arrival. It was at this point in the life of Jesus that the records clearly state who Jesus was, what He was to do: "the Lamb of God who takes away the sin of the world!" (John 1:29.)

Jesus was the Man in whom we saw God fully revealed. He used powers no mere man could have possessed. Ordinary men do ordinary things; unusual men do the unusual; extraordinary men do extraordinary things in the eyes of men—but all according to the talents with which God has endowed them, each in harmony with his own particular mission, be it ordinary or extraordinary.

The "works" of Jesus are in keeping with His character of Messiah. All that He was, all that He is, Jesus put and puts at the service of humanity. He was and is divine Love-made-Man, doing all that love can do. For love must dare the worst and do the most! What Jesus felt, He means for us to feel; the way He served, He means for us to serve, and the way He loved, He means for us to love!

It is shocking to note that a vast majority of people who call themselves Christians give no thought to bringing about better understanding and improved living conditions in society. It should also be noted that just as soon as any man earnestly attacks the problems of improving living conditions for the disadvantaged, he immediately understands why the symbol of the Christian religion is the Cross.

With Jesus "the kingdom of God" was something more than an eruption of mysterious forces from the invisible world which would upset and transform world order. With Jesus the kingdom was a present reality. Jesus was concerned far more about a "new creature" than about a "new creation." In other words, He believed that you should refine the gift you have been given and work to perfect it. This is you, endowed with the talent and grace that God gave you, that I speak of over and over. Use that talent of yours and the divine assistance that accompanies it. It is important, most of all for yourself, but also for humanity.

Someday we will not be just "one nation under God" but "one *world* under God." Jesus was concerned for the world He knew would evolve. He was teaching, not to bring about a transformed physical universe, but to transform human hearts and minds that they might build the kingdom of God in the faithful—those who would follow Him, like you and me.

Not one among the teachers of that time had any idea other than that the Messiah would be a temporal Messiah who would set up the kingdom of plenty in which "the hungry were to be filled with good things." What so many do not realize is the truth of the word of Jesus that we must first love God above all things. They are unaware that this is religion pure and simple. For if one loves God—truly loves Him—he must fulfill the second part of Jesus' word and love his neighbor. Why? Because he will see in his neighbor the irresistible image of his God!

The Gospel shows the birth of Jesus to have been the fulfillment of prophecy (Micah 5:1). Jesus Himself had

the divine gift of foretelling the future (Luke 21:6-33).
He saw the progress of science far into the future—to our
own day and still to come.

Historical research has given us the clear description
of Jesus the Man. "The Holy Shroud of Turin," so-
called because it is preserved in that Italian city, has
been accepted on scientific grounds, joining religion, history, and science.

Microscopic studies were made of the burial cloth,
giving pure scientific proof of its existence after more
than two years of study and research. The circumstances
of its discovery and the accounts of Christ's death were
also scientifically verified. Checked by "vaporography,"
the shroud has been identified by experts as the genuine
burial winding sheet of Christ. From this also we are
given a physical description of the Man. Jesus weighed
about one hundred and seventy pounds. Well propor-
tioned, He was five feet eleven, considered very tall for
His day. Despite the bruises—evidence of nail indenta-
tions in the wrist bones, one spike driven through
crossed feet, a shaped crown of thorns, side-wound
gashes and back wounds from scourging—we find Jesus
had well-defined features in a classic masculine face. He
was strong and robust, genuinely noble and impressive in
appearance. Only a man of such compelling stature and
forceful physique could have broken free from the Nazarene crowd that tried to throw Him from a cliff, or
single-handedly attacked money changers in the temple
and driven them out, or walked the length and breadth
of Palestine, often spending whole nights in prayer.

Such a man could survive a Roman scourging that was
known throughout Judea as "the intermediary death,"
then have the horizontal beam of a heavy wooden cross
strapped to His arms and shoulders, carrying it an as-
tonishing distance, uphill all the way.

His was no stained-glass figure with sweety-sweet
countenance. In order to be the eternal Christ, Jesus had

first to be a human being. He suffered and experienced feelings like other mortals. He suffered fatigue, exhaustion, hunger, loneliness, sorrow, longing, as well as great joy and exaltation.

A Roman official, Publius Lentulus, in a routine report addressed to Caesar and the Roman senate, writes:

> In these our days appeared a man named Jesus Christ, who yet lives among us, and is accepted as a great prophet of truth by the Gentiles. But His own disciples called Him the Son of God. He has raised the dead and cured all manner of diseases. He is a man of stature somewhat tall and comely, with a ruddy countenance such as one might both love and fear. His hair is the color of a ripe filbert, plain to the ear. It falls down to his shoulders where it is more of an orient color. In the middle of His head is a seam of long hair, after the manner of the Nazarites. His forehead is plain and delicate, the face without blemish or wrinkle, beautiful and comely; His nose and mouth are exactly formed. His beard is the color of His hair and thick, not of much length, but forked.
>
> In reproving He is terrible; in admonishing courteous; in speaking, very modest and wise. His body is well-shaped and well-proportioned. None have seen Him laugh; many have seen Him weep. As a man he surpasses in excellence the children of men.

Along with His strength Jesus was unfailingly sensitive and gentle. In everything, in every way, He tried to teach men to seek love and wisdom greater than their own, that they might grapple with and conquer the demands made upon them daily by the circumstances of their lives.

"God blessed them, saying: 'Be fertile and multiply; fill the earth and subdue it.'" (Genesis 1:28.)

God did not create and place us here on earth for us to use others for our own selfish purposes, but to serve Him and benefit one another.

—Jeane Dixon

2. The Divine Design

It is God's master plan for each one of His creatures to do its own thing, that is, for the cell to grow and continue to multiply, the plant to flourish and reseed through the processes of Nature, and man to learn and develop through his faith in God and the full use of his foreordained talents and abilities.

It is not the kind of talent He has given you in His Divine Design but *what you do with it* that is important.

For if you are using your talent to the very best of your ability and are in spiritual harmony with your Creator and fellow man through faith, then you are doing great things in the eyes of God, no matter how men may evaluate your achievements.

For the best part of any life is not necessarily its achievements, its successes, its triumphs in the eyes of men. These are often costly, delayed, or even bitter, like the dregs of vintage wine. The best memories of any life, as of any journey, do not always begin at the beginning; but the best parts are more likely to occur somewhere in midcareer when things are going well and you are lost in the heady promises of new horizons, expanding dreams, glorious expectations.

The life of Jesus was humble in its beginnings, meteoric in its rise, unparalleled in its greatness, but in one sense, infinitely tragic in its conclusion, though all Western history was to be its epilogue. Jesus' happiest hours were, no doubt, spent on quiet Sabbath afternoons with Mary and Joseph in the realization of His divine identity and mission, or with Martha and Mary in Bethany after a week of tramping the hills and roads of Galilee.

There were many such days in His early life. Later on, however, His hours of rest and recreation were filled with crowds, preaching sermons on a mount or from the back of a boat, eyes burning with prophetic vision, His words plumbing infinite depths of God's wisdom, knowledge and love. "No man ever spoke like that before." (John 7:46.)

George Ferry in his painting *Christ Arousing His Disciples* has captured an informal but eternal moment in the Master's life that was undoubtedly one of the most pleasant. He is seen from the side, walking through a field at leisure with three of His apostles. One is lying in the grass on his stomach, another on his back gazing up at the sky, while the third is kneeling as he listens to immortal words cascading from the Messiah's lips. It was one of those sunny afternoons of life He must have enjoyed most as a man of His time, far from the shadow of the Roman Empire, the Sanhedrin, and the Cross. Days like this add up to the best things in life.

It was on such a day in such a scene that Christ told His apostles to seek first the Kingdom of God, to love God above all things, their neighbors as themselves, and to worship God in spirit and in truth. "Anyone committed to the truth hears my voice," He told the world through Pontius Pilate. (John 18:37.) To those who loved Him better He had said: "I am the way, and the truth, and the life" (John 14:6), explaining God's Divine Design for individuals so it could be understood and carried on by the apostles then and by each one of us now.

All life, all education, all human relations are founded on this divine plan. God founded the world according to this divine plan.

America, too, was founded on basic religious principles. Our Constitution, Declaration of Independence, and Bill of Rights written by our founding fathers read in part like a Mosaic tract. The fidelity of these founders and the devotion of our people to God's truth, our freedom to seek it out and live by its standards, have been the great and controlling reasons for our spectacular rise to unparalleled power in less than two centuries. History may never again see the like. Indeed, it cannot, for the conditions are no longer available on this planet.

But what a long spiral downward we have seen since the end of World War II! How justified our people are in their apprehensions that something has gone wrong in our nation's spirit, something that is not traceable merely to demonstrators, radicals, and some uninformed youth!

It is a certain sickness of the soul of which all of us have been aware, somehow, some way. During the time between our military stalemate in Korea and our loss of faith in the cause of Vietnam, have we openly retreated from our traditional beliefs in the ideals of truth and justice?

As the case of the secret Vietnam papers published in *The New York Times* and *Washington Post* was on its way to the Supreme Court, the *Post* published a cartoon portraying our "new secret weapon" as the big lie. Another cartoon in *Newsday* showed "Top Secret" as a way around Lincoln's dictum about fooling all of the people all of the time. What is happening to us?

Are we, a country dedicated to certain "self-evident truths," becoming a nation of liars?

Are we losing our love of the truth by allowing our leaders to lie to us and letting them get away with it?

From campaign promises to the permissible lies of

advertising that keep our free press going, we have learned to live with a certain expectation and tolerance of less than the truth. We allow our leadership and those who serve us to betray our better judgment with flattery and fables. Really, the Pentagon Papers should have surprised no one. Governments have been lying to their people for centuries, but it is only now that we have become so powerful that the consequences have become so terrible. Only in our lifetime has it become possible to destroy the world's largest cities simply by pressing buttons thousands of miles away. Only since 1945 have the forces of death become so formidable that they seriously threaten the survival of life. They need only a continuation of secrecy, lying, and intrigue to succeed.

The Pentagon Papers, for all their bulk and melodrama, added very little beyond confirming details of what we already knew: the "secret" was in Laos and North Vietnam in 1964 before the public was officially informed, the Tonkin Gulf incident that was used so provocatively, the gradual escalation of war by men pledging themselves publicly to "peace," the American preoccupation with image building and making ourselves look and feel good, and the promises of success after the next "turn of the screw."

I tried to warn our country and its leaders about all this and more every time I spoke. I wrote in *My Life and Prophecies*, published in 1969. "For years now in the face of optimistic pronouncements by our high officials, I have seen the ghastly specter of death and destruction in Vietnam. In every speech I have made during the past few years, I have stated that this war would continue, despite the auspicious reports to the nations by politicians and generals. I saw, and still see, more American blood being shed on the battlefields. I have always tied the future of Vietnam and Korea together, for politically they are one and the same problem."

I saw this a long time before these words were written, before we were bogged down in Vietnam. Back in 1963 when Madam Nhu came to America seeking our government's help, I wrote to the then President Kennedy outlining the only course that would save us from our present tragic failure in Southeast Asia. The key to securing Vietnam from Communist domination and to keeping it from falling behind the iron curtain lay in backing the regime of President Ngo Dinh Diem during the Kennedy-Johnson years. The contents of this plan were publicized by Madame Nhu and consisted mainly of economic aid with a limited officer corps to train the Vietnamese army. The essence of the plan was to back the going Diem Government, leaving the running of it in their hands. But the "government within a government" of which I also wrote at that time would have none of this plan. I know that President Kennedy favored the plan, but when he presented it to his advisors, his opinion was overruled. And there went our last chance for an honorable, economical, and peaceful solution to the dilemma of Southeast Asia.

President Kennedy still favored the plan, but he was already in serious difficulty with the "government within a government" as we saw in the Bay of Pigs fiasco, and he evidently did not feel secure enough to press ahead single-handedly on his own. If only he had!

But there are forces at work in history beyond the control of even the greatest men, and the destiny of nations can depend upon the erroneous belief of one critical figure among a ruler's advisors. The erroneous knowledge used at this time was that President Diem kept Saigon much too tightly controlled for liberal American democratic sensitivities. But the next time President Kennedy left Washington the same well-intentioned advisors inadvertently committed a shameful and infamous deed, of which the Pentagon Papers leave a confirmed and incontrovertible record.

I was glad that Senator Edward Kennedy desired a

complete investigation and revelation of all the mistakes and deceptions of the Vietnamese tragedy, even those involving members of his own family, a truly heroic gesture. For the man whose youthful enthusiasm could never quite come to grips with the hard core of reality, whose erroneous information extinguished our last chance for effective action in Vietnam, was a member of his family.

Through my everlasting faith in my own God-given talent I felt I had much to offer the Kennedy family, and through them our country and the world. But somehow my friendly overtures to them have always been met with a mystifying rejection. This is hurtful, because as stated before, some of the most powerful vibrations I have ever received were intended to help the Kennedys help the world!

One of the first things President Johnson did upon taking office was to call in the architects of the Vietnam disaster and try to salvage something intelligent and defensible from the mess they had made. He was especially angry about the assassination of President Diem, whose problems he was about to inherit. With Diem gone, the Saigon Government was going to pieces, coup by coup, just as Madame Nhu had said it would.

Like his predecessor, President Johnson was confronted by the "government within a government," which itself began to fragment. But it was already too late to save South Vietnam. A few months previously, while President Kennedy was out of Washington, a State Department official gave the "green light" for the end of President Diem. Of course this official did not act solely on his own authority. The Pentagon Papers link a presidential advisor who sent the fatal cable and an ambassador who was to deliver what amounted to a sentence of execution. As one of the news magazines remarked, "That was inexcusable."

The other men President Johnson called to account

fare little better at the hands of an unfolding, impartial history: the human computer whose particular tragedy was that he was more computer than human; the benevolent despot who thought he could impose freedom on people who had no understanding of what he meant by the word; the man with delusions of omnipotence, who thought you could do anything by pressing buttons and firing guns; the man who believed you should stick by your mistakes instead of correcting them; and all the other clever "little office boys" who played with power while the boss was out.

The "government within a government" became so confused and contradictory, so uncontrollable and disastrous, that President Johnson ultimately gave up and chose not to run in 1968. I am sure he felt sincerely he could do more for his country serving in other capacities.

While Lyndon Baines Johnson was in the White House, I tried to warn him repeatedly that his dependence upon his advisors would be a mistake—that he should carry his own image and opinions and not try to second-guess his predecessor. Unfortunately he was trapped in the Vietnamese War and remained trapped during his administration because of injudicious informants who continued counseling him to ignore the Russian role in Vietnam.

I still see ex-President Johnson growing in stature as a result of the Pentagon Papers, because he is now free to devote his energies, talents, and influence toward correcting the blunders of the past decades.

As for the others, I cannot agree with the common assessment that they were just poor but honest men of limited vision, trying to find the best solution to an impossible problem. Hardly honorable men defending the orthodoxies of another time, their trouble was that they never once thought of defending the great orthodoxy of all time, the integrity of moral truth!

They left that to others. We have "a tragedy without

villains, war crimes without criminals, and lies without liars" in a tragic farce that puts procedures above principles, expediency before justice, and political power ahead of the public interest.

Where there is no vision, the people perish. They have been perishing in Vietnam now for over a decade, Americans and Asians alike, because there was no guiding vision of truth, justice, and love. Instead, as the Pentagon Papers show, there was only shallow egotism, deceptive double-talk, and honest bewilderment.

As our leaders sat around long mahogany tables in sophisticated poses deciding the fate of nations and armies, they looked like great men of wisdom and courage; but even a brief look behind the scenes confirmed what we should have realized all along: they were men whose power exceeded their capabilities, whose mistakes exceeded their wisdom, and whose lack of vision was almost incredible.

Well might the words of Jesus be applied to those unvisionaries who ignored Madame Nhu's plea: "Father, Lord of heaven and earth . . . what you have hidden from the learned and the clever you have revealed to the merest children." (Matthew 11:25.)

We, the people, are learning ever so slowly and painfully that war is a nasty business and that it must be stopped, not by trickery and deception, but by honesty in human affairs, whether personal or political. Men and women just cannot be dealt with as if they were pawns in a power game, to be exterminated, rewarded, punished, or glorified at will. They are not merely to be used or manipulated in large numbers like an audience under the control of a dramatist. They are creatures of God, brothers and sisters to be helped, served and worked with as opportunity affords . . . meaning that we should use our divinely granted talents for the benefit of others and not to dominate and control them.

This is the oldest American ideal, derived from a

religious faith thousands of years old. It seems to be in eclipse now, and that is the source of our trouble. If we betray it now for an image of ourselves derived from computer games and systems analyses—the placement of power and prestige above personality and principle—then we shall help to turn the world of the future into a much worse mess than Vietnam. But if we seek the truth of God's divine design and the love of man with all our hearts, we can yet prove worthy of the tremendous trust God has invested in us!

"I will make you a light to the nations, that my salvation may reach to the ends of the earth." (Isaiah 49:6.)

The fulfillment of Isaiah's prophecy is still to come . . . and fortunately for all of us it will come.

—Jeane Dixon

3. The Prophets and the Promise

Great decisions in history, like the momentous one Jesus made, usually pass unnoticed in their own time. They appear in the perspective of a later time, when some author or artist looks back through the eyes of genius ferreting out the historic decisions of destiny: *Paul on the Road to Damascus, Aristotle Contemplating the Bust of Homer, Washington at Valley Forge,* Salvador Dali giving us new symbolism in *The Last Supper* and *The Crucifixion!*

These are signposts of the centuries along the highroad of human history. They are the magnificent illustrations in the continuing story of mankind. The text itself has been inscribed by men who could not possibly have appreciated the stature of their greatness. It was Chaucer who interpreted the thrust of his time and determined the future of the English language by using it instead of the courtly French or classic Latin then fashionable in London society. It was Shakespeare who later paved the way for the British Empire by dramatizing what England had in common with Rome and Egypt, awakening his country's appetite for grandeur. It was really Samuel Beckett who penetrated most deeply into the emptiness and futility of a faithless society by dramatizing its enslavement to nothingness.

But when did Chaucer decide to write in English and

thus establish the most prolific literary medium for centuries to come? When did Shakespeare decide that the King Henry portrayals and Julius Caesar had something in common? Just what compelled Beckett to depict an outworn culture tirelessly waiting for death?

Like the fateful decisions of individuals, such moments of great consequence for humanity are clothed in layers of secret meditation and self-communing, far beneath the level of conscious thought. Alexander, Napoleon, Abraham Lincoln, if pressed to analyze their thought processes in moments of great decision, would probably muse and ponder the question, with interesting sidelights on our current concepts of their times and roles.

But concerning the greatest Character in all history, there is no doubt about the fateful moment of self-revelation. It came on a Sabbath Day nearly two thousand years ago in the little town of Nazareth as the Carpenter, Jesus, stood up to read from the Book of Isaiah.

"The Spirit of the Lord is upon me," He began, "therefore he has anointed me. He has sent me to bring glad tidings to the poor, to proclaim liberty to captives, recovery of sight to the blind and release to prisoners, to announce a year of favor from the Lord." (Luke 4: 18-19.)

"Rolling up the scroll he gave it back to the assistant and sat down." There was silence in the synagogue, all eyes fixed upon Him, for they sensed that this was no ordinary Sabbath. Then Jesus stood up and announced: "Today this Scripture passage is fulfilled in your hearing." (Luke 4:20-21.)

His hearers were astounded!

For many centuries the people of Israel had awaited the promised Messiah. Generation after generation had repeated the words of the ancient prophets, over and over again. Could it possibly be true that this neighbor of theirs, the humble carpenter, son of Joseph, was indeed He of whom Isaiah had spoken? Indeed, did Jesus Himself at that moment know that winning their confidence would lead Him to the Cross on Good Friday?

Most of the V.I.P.'s in the Old Testament were prophets, not kings—Isaiah, Jeremiah, Ezekiel, Samson, Eli, Samuel, Daniel, Elijah. Following the virtual disintegration of Israel after the glorious reign of King Solomon, the voice of the prophet became increasingly influential throughout the land. One of the recurring prophecies concerned a divine leader who would appear and restore Israel to greatness. Century after century prophet after prophet advanced the promise, so that by the time of Herod's cruel reign a veritable frenzy of expectation gripped the land.

Isaiah, whose name means "Salvation of God," was the most notable of the prophets, and may have been the mightiest seer who ever lived.

Isaiah was born about the year 760 B.C. and lived to be a very old man. Three generations of Hebrews listened to his words, for he was a powerful preacher, whose interests were without limit. Statesman and advisor to kings, he was the man of his time as well as a man of all time. We know little of the day-to-day existence of Isaiah, but the grandeur, inspiration, and wisdom that shine through his works combine with his insight to assure him a place of exalted leadership among the Israelite people and their prophets.

Isaiah appeared during a critical period of Hebrew history. Northern Israel had collapsed under the pressure of the mighty Assyrian Empire and the army of Sennacherib came down like a wolf on the fold to the very walls of Jerusalem itself. In desperation the king sought to enlist the aid of Egypt, which Isaiah denounced as a betrayal of Israel. The Prophet blamed the ills of the time on the decadence and infidelity of the people, including the priests and king. Revitalized faith in the God of Israel alone would save the people. Isaiah preached, and at length they believed him. Sennacherib, after boasting that he had shut up the King of Israel like a "bird in his cage," was forced to retreat from the Gates of Jerusalem.

Yet throughout, the prophet Isaiah inspired the people with hope for the coming of the Messiah and His salvation. The people could see only death and desolation in their future, caught as they were between Assyria and Egypt. They had escaped the bondage of the Pharaoh only to become slaves of the Assyrians. The days of King David and King Solomon were taunting memories. The present was bleak; the future looked even worse. Yahweh had apparently abandoned them; why not give other gods a try?

Israel became God's problem child.

But there was the certainty of forgiveness . . . the preparation for things to come . . . so even in the face of this new threat Isaiah stood fast.

Isaiah was a complete man of God, which is to say he was a total man with a key to history.

"O Lord, you are my God, I will extol you and praise your name" (Isaiah 25:1), he promised.

He longed for the peace of God, but his lifetime vision that people "shall beat their swords into plowshares and their spears into pruning hooks; one nation shall not raise the sword against another, nor shall they train for war again" (Isaiah 2:4) was just that—a vision of the distant future.

These words of Isaiah (which reappear in Micah 4:3), are inscribed on a wall at the United Nations in New York, but we are as far from peace as the men of his time, except, of course, in the chronological sense.

The fulfillment of Isaiah's prophecy, like many others, is still to come—and fortunately, it will come.

For then, as now, came God's promise of redemption with the coming of the Messiah prophesied by Isaiah.

There is an awesome quality about Isaiah's revelation of Jesus' life and death; he even touches upon the scourging and our Savior's silence before Pilate. "He was spurned and avoided by men, a man of suffering, accustomed to infirmity, one of those from whom men hide their faces. . . . But he was pierced for our offenses, crushed for our sins, upon him was the chastisement that makes us whole, by his stripes we were healed . . . Though he was harshly treated, he submitted and opened not his mouth; like a lamb led to the slaughter or a sheep before the shearers, he was silent and opened not his mouth. Oppressed and condemned, he was taken away, and who would have thought any more of his destiny? When he was cut off from the land of the living, and smitten for the sin of his people . . . Because he surrendered himself to death and was counted among the wicked . . . he shall take away the sins of many, and win pardon for their offenses." (Isaiah 53:3-12.)

The term *win pardon* is used in relation to Jesus as mediator. This later becomes a matter of dogma in Christian faith—Christ the Mediator with God. In the Letter of Paul to the Romans, we read: "Christ Jesus, who died or rather was raised up, who is at the right hand of God and who intercedes for us." (Romans 8:34.)

Isaiah and the other prophets prepared the way for Jesus. Many Jews did accept Him as the Lord their God, but the people of Israel placed their own interpretation on the prophetic writings. Instead of a "Prince of Peace," they looked rather for a Joshua or a David, a leader who would smash their enemies as before and restore the glorious days. It was precisely this misguided dream of forceful victory that destroyed them, for it led to the *Diaspora*, or "dispersion" of the Jews, the Roman version of the "final solution."

Jesus was to be a leader, the greatest of all time, but He would fulfill the prophecies in a universal sense rather than the provincial concept of a local or regional hero.

The advent of the unified world was dawning. His message was to bring the revelation of God "to every creature." Isaiah keeps insisting on this point: "All the ends of the earth will behold the salvation of our God." (Isaiah 52:10.) We understand from this that nothing less than unity of religion under one God can satisfy the needs of humanity.

I am especially interested in the Old Testament prophets as they relate to the coming of Jesus, the Messiah. What is this gift of prophecy that maintains a continuing communication between God and man? We know that God has alwavs revealed Himself to men in one way or another. In ancient times it was thought to be through the supernatural, the response to God's call and the subsequent careers of Abraham and Moses, or of Joshua at the conquest of Canaan. God always reveals Himself as a *presence*, but not like the portrayals of the Divine in literature, drama, and art. God's link with the Old Testament world was chiefly through the prophets, devoted men whose Creator had bestowed upon them the gift of prophecy and whose prayerful spirit of deep meditation enabled them to receive communications of God's knowledge beyond the reach of others. Such prophets usually appeared during times of great crises or of straying from God's Commandments—there are ten of them, known as the Decalogue (Exodus 20:1-17).

It is my belief God has given me a gift of prophecy for His own reasons, and I do not question them. To me, prayer is never a monotonous burden of repetition, a pious exhibition of vocalizing; rather it is a wondrous way of "talking to God." Somehow I know He listens. With added periods of meditation, reflection, and inter-pretation it becomes, for me at least, joy beyond all telling!

At such times I develop a degree of concentration that

shuts out all distractions of the surrounding world and makes way for the Divine Presence. I empty my mind in order that I may be filled with the Spirit of God. Finally, during my meditations, when my spirit is calm and He is ready, God talks to me.

I know then, beyond all doubt, that the channel is coming directly to me from the Divine, the Lord our God, because I feel it and sense it. I know it is not the channel of Satan, because his channel I have felt and sensed too; and I definitely know the difference. So according to my wisdom I follow the Lord's channel, because that is my Lord's will.

My reading of Scripture assures me that this is the way it was with the biblical prophets. They put their trust in God totally and without reservation, and God in turn freely chose them for the gift of prophecy. He entrusted them with the hidden knowledge of their time and the coming of His Son among men.

Each of the prophets in turn prophesied a part of God's plan, always coming nearer to its fulfillment. Micah, a contemporary of Isaiah, turned to prophecy late in life and directed the attention of his people from the great truths of Isaiah to the smaller details of the Messiah's birthplace and the splendor of His reign. But "you, Bethlehem-Ephrathah, too small to be among the clans of Judah, from you shall come forth for me one who is to be ruler in Israel . . . from ancient times." (Micah 5:1.)

The phrase *from ancient times*, that is, everlastingly, is filled with significance. The life of Jesus on earth was not the beginning of His existence; the roots of His being are with God in the divine Trinity, with no beginning and no end. The historical Jesus was born in Bethlehem, as Micah foretold, of a human mother, Mary; but in and through His divine nature He is also one with God. In Saint John's gospel He is asked: "Surely you do not pretend to be greater than our father Abraham, who died! Or the prophets, who died! Whom do you make yourself out to be?"

Jesus answers: "Your father Abraham rejoiced that he might see my day. He saw it and was glad."

Then the Jews objected: "You are not yet fifty! How can you have seen Abraham?"

"I solemnly declare it," Jesus answered them, "before Abraham came to be, I AM." (John 8:53, 56-58.)

On another occasion he went further, saying: "The Father and I are one." (John 10:30.)

The prophecy of Zechariah foretells an event with curious implications: the entry of Jesus into Jerusalem on Palm Sunday. "Rejoice heartily, O daughter Zion, shout for joy, O daughter Jerusalem! See, your king shall come to you; a just savior is he, meek, and riding on an ass." (Zechariah 9:9.)

It was the destiny of the prophecy of Malachi, in the fifth century B.C., to close out the Old Testament, and to do so with a flourish. For it was this prophecy which announced the coming of the Messiah and also of His precursor, John the Baptist, who reincarnated the spirit and power of Elijah and completed his mission: "Lo, I am sending my messenger to prepare the way before me; and suddenly there will come to the temple the Lord whom you seek" . . . and again, "I will send you Elijah, the prophet, before the day of the Lord comes, the great and terrible day, to turn the hearts of the fathers to their children, and the hearts of the children to their fathers." (Malachi 3:1, 23-24.)

These are the prophecies of the ancients about the coming "great and terrible day of the lord," and I recommend them to the men and women of our time.

" 'I assure you, though, that Elijah has already come, but they did not recognize him and they did as they pleased with him.' . . . . The disciples then realized that he had been speaking to them about John the Baptizer." (Matthew 17:12-13.)

We shall see the beginnings of Christ's apocalyptic reentry into this world's history in the next half-century.

—Jeane Dixon

4. "Elijah Is Come Already"

Was John the Baptist truly the reincarnation of the spirit of Elijah?

We have the word of Jesus that he was!

On the night of the Transfiguration as Peter, James, and John accompanied Jesus down from the mountaintop, they questioned Him on this point. "Why do the scribes claim that Elijah must come first?" they asked Him.

In reply Jesus said: " 'I assure you, though, that Elijah has already come, but they did not recognize him and they did as they pleased with him. The Son of Man will suffer at their hands the same way.' The disciples then realized that he had been speaking to them about John the Baptizer." (Matthew 17:10-13.)

This was not the only time that Jesus spoke of the spirit of Elijah reincarnated in John. In Chapter Eleven of the Gospel according to Matthew we read: "From John the Baptizer's time until now the kingdom of God has suffered violence, and the violent take it by force. All the prophets as well as the law spoke prophetically until John. If you are prepared to accept it, he is Elijah, the one who was certain to come." (Matthew 11:12-14.)

Also, Saint Luke in his first chapter, announcing to Zechariah the birth of the Baptizer, says of him: "God himself will go before him, in the spirit and power of Elijah." (Luke 1:17.)

"In the spirit and power of Elijah." This is the key to a correct understanding of the phenomenon. There is endless fascination with the subject of reincarnation, and I deal specifically with the phase of it in my book *My Life and Prophecies*. However, in order to correct misunderstandings and make my views completely clear, I later published a little volume titled *Reincarnation and Prayers To Live By*, developing more fully this subject.

There is much confusion about reincarnation and what it means. The most frequently asked question is: what happens to one's soul in the process of reincarnation? Does the person who has passed on lose his soul when the spirit is reincarnated into another soul and body?

The answer lies in understanding the difference between what is meant by "soul" and what is meant by "spirit." The soul (*psyche* in Greek, *anima* in Latin) is the "life principle" in man. When united with a body of flesh, it makes man a living being. It is individual, singular, spiritual, and never reincarnated in another body. It is the subject of personal life. Your "soul" is your consciousness or identity, which remains after death and, if it lived in conformity to the will of God, enters into the life of God forever.

Spirit (Greek, *pneuma*; Latin, *spiritus*) refers to the center of mental activities. It is not restricted to the individual, but may live on and on. It is this quality that is reincarnated, or continued in other souls, to go through the life cycle at the right time in accordance with God's plan for us to carry on a particular mission at a precise time in the history of men.

Removed in time nine centuries from one another, the spirit of Elijah appeared again in John the Baptizer, just as perhaps the spirit of Orlando di Lasso may have reappeared in the boy Mozart, or the spirit of Saint Francis in Albert Schweitzer or Florence Nightingale.

Elijah and John were imbued with an essentially crusading spirit: Elijah to restore Israel to its divine religious faith; John the Baptizer, in his own words, quoting the prophet Isaiah: "A herald's voice in the desert: 'Prepare the way of the Lord, make straight his paths.' " (Matthew 3:3.)

The similarity of their lives is striking: Elijah was persecuted by the licentious Queen Jezebel, and John by the weak and flabby King Herod through another licentious queen, Herodias, and her daughter Salome. Both prophets were overzealous children of the desert, clothed in animal skins and eating what they could scavenge from nature, reprimanding kings and condemning the rulers of Israel for leading the people astray.

Elijah saved his people from renouncing their covenant with God, while John prepared the way for the Messiah.

It seems to me that there is need today for a return of the spirit of Elijah and John the Baptist: Elijah to bring our self-destructing citizens back to their covenant with God—our Creator—and John to prepare the way for our return to Jesus!

If the spirit of Elijah was really incarnate in John—as it was—should not the same spirit be reincarnated today to "prepare the way" for the greatest religious event in modern times?

It is coming!

I have said before, and I say again: we shall see the beginnings of Christ's apocalyptic reentry into this world's history in the next half-century. Note well: I said "the beginnings" ... that is, the approach of the prophet of the Antichrist, not the fulfillment of *all* the prophecies in Chapter Twenty-four of Saint Matthew, which will come at a later time.

In Chapter Nine of *My Life and Prophecies* I wrote of "The Coming of the Antichrist," and in Chapter Ten,

"The Child From the East." I am now ready to go a step further.

A short time ago it was revealed to me that the masses of people whom I saw at the forked road in "the valley of decision" described in Chapter Ten are unfortunately being prepared and tragically are preparing themselves to follow the "Child of the East" to the left. "The gate that leads to damnation is wide, the road is clear, and many choose to travel it. But how narrow is the gate that leads to life, how rough the road, and how few there are who find it." (Matthew 7:13-14.)

In a vision I saw this embodied symbolically in the act of Pontius Pilate washing his hands of the condemnation of Jesus.

A vision appeared—and in this vision I was standing alone in the desert. I looked to my left, and there was a prison. In the vision I knew without being told that Barabbas was imprisoned there; he was not one of the robbers crucified on a cross beside Jesus, but a thief and a murderer.

Then, looking straight ahead, I saw Pontius Pilate sitting on a chair that was elevated. It was not a throne, but a very important-looking chair, a chair to be used only by one in authority.

I turned my gaze to the right, where hills rose from the plain, and saw someone walking very slowly down the hillside toward us. At the foot of the hill He stopped on a grassy knoll and looked out over the desert. I saw the grass had turned brown beneath His feet as He stood, and I knew that this was Jesus.

Again, I turned to the left; somehow a huge crowd of people had assembled where at first there had been only the prison.

Wondering, I looked again at Pontius Pilate sitting in the elevated chair. He was saying: "You shall make the decision . . . you shall make the decision."

The crowd shouted back as with one voice: "Free

Barabbas! Free Barabbas! Persecute Jesus! Persecute Jesus!"

Replying, Pontius Pilate again twice repeated his words: "You have made the decision ... you have made the decision. Free Barabbas ... free Barabbas!"

But he did not say, "Persecute Jesus!"

Sadly, I turned to my left. I saw Barabbas freed from the prison, whereupon he led the people to the left between the prison and the chair of Pontius Pilate. He continued to lead the people, and in my vision they trampled over other people, over buildings, over heads of state, over government structures, and everything in their pathway was left in utter shambles.

At last I saw a lighted steeple, a small steeple pointing heavenward, atop a church. It seemed like a beacon in the darkness—but it was also destroyed by the mob.

Once more I heard the voice of Pontius Pilate, "When the evil of one man can lead the masses to destruction, then no longer can the majority rule the earth or the Church!"

Loudly he repeated it: "When the evil of one man can lead the masses to destruction, then no longer can the majority rule the earth or the Church!"

Silence descended on the desert—a silence so loud you could hear its stillness. In that awful, ominous silence came another voice, from above me, from in back of me, from in front, from all around, it came pleading: "Follow me ... follow me ... follow me!"

But the people of the mob paid no attention. They kept following the same as before and headed toward the Antichrist ... it was Barabbas who led them.

It is my belief that we are now in a state akin to that time just before John began baptizing in the Jordan. The fragmenting Church is likened to those crowds of people, bereft of effective leadership in their church, who went out to the Jordan to find the Spirit of God in

John. Instead of baptism today there is a kind of mass brainwashing going on, both within and without the Church, by which people are being robbed of their religious heritage. The agitators, infiltrators, and student radicals have done their work well! So have the philosophers of social revolution and the "death-of-God" theologians, until there is hardly any substance left. With "educators" acting like juveniles it is only logical that the young demand positions of authority and responsibility that have been abdicated. The stability of family life decays as more and more parents succumb to the years of quiet desperation.

As the demoralization of the young goes on it seems inevitable that they might reject the image of life retained from their earliest years and seek out possible scapegoats and alternatives. Surely there is a sound basis for saying something is wrong with diplomacy that leads to war, with science that achieves greater and greater possibilities of nuclear horror, with industry and transportation that soon may pollute us out of existence! So intense is the bitterness of some that they now threaten to reject humanity itself in a return to tribal and instinctual primitive living.

To the most intense it seems everything drives them into that path. They see art that has become elemental, literature that has become schizoid and paranoiac, music a welter of "sound and fury signifying nothing." The things that should refresh and console them do not! Wherever they look, to whomever they turn, the bitter young find little more than empty rationalizations, futile disbelief, and small hope. They are "turned off," as they say, by the sight of barbaric war on the one hand, and noble pretensions on the other. "Honesty and sincerity," their cardinal virtues, are casualties of rhetoric. To them the Establishment seems all-powerful, hobbling along on repression and hypocrisy. How sad they will not realize that if only they joined the Establishment, instead of opposing it, by working they could begin to effect some of the changes that they are now only demonstrating for.

It is small wonder that the young and lately young are growing into a group that will soon be a dissident majority. Why should they not follow any leader who offers them escape from what they think are intolerable conditions of life? And not only escape, but hope, for a world more to their liking?

Without true faith, spiritual hope, or genuine love, they will be ripe for a revolution that will make Marxism seem pious!

Along with the rest of us they have been conditioned by a descending spiral of infidelity. We are victims of a brainwashing that has been going on for centuries. Just as the Chosen People of old had their true prophets periodically calling them to attention in preparation for Christ's coming, so have we had our antiprophets for the past millennium to prepare us for the coming of the Antichrist.

Beginning with the Eastern revolt and the Crusades which followed, and going on through the Renaissance and the Reformation, there is the undeniable rationale of individual and national sovereignty that has led to two world wars, with a third now brewing. Evidenced by a materialistic philosophy, a godless science, and a skeptical cynicism in morals, the present course of Western civilization was studied and foreseen by Arnold Toynbee with all its implications long before it became fashionable to quote him in intellectual circles or refute his latest theory.

"The sun of death," the mushroom cloud, that rose in the Pacific skies in 1945 and ever since has grown more dazzling, was a predictable outcome of using human ingenuity without *divine restraint*. So are the coming events I am now predicting, unless a return to Jesus makes His visitation to us for "punishment" unnecessary.

I see the dawn of a new Good Friday looming over the historic hill.

To face the tests now confronting us we need a new Transfiguration to inspire us with spiritual courage and faith in God. Instead of revolutions by the masses we need a transformation of the individual from within. We need to be free of pollution in every aspect and accept life as a reality—using our divinely granted gifts to build rather than to destroy!

In the spirit of Elijah I say: If God be God, then acknowledge Him and honor His law! Recognize that He has declared Himself a God of love and not of holocausts. With John the Baptist I say: "Make ready the way of the Lord, clear him a straight path. Every valley shall be filled and every mountain and hill shall be leveled. The windings shall be made straight and the rough ways smooth, and all mankind shall see the salvation of God." (Luke 3:4-6.)

But it will not come about in an easy, comfortable, agreeable way. The span of man's ferocity in history will increase in our time. We must prove ourselves worthy of the age of peace and goodwill that is still half a century away. It will burst upon us with the splendor of a longed-for Christmas, but it will be preceded by the long Lent of enforced deprivation and preparation of which I have spoken.

"After Jesus was baptized, he came directly out of the water. Suddenly the sky opened and he saw the Spirit of God descend like a dove and hover over him. With that, a voice from the heavens said, 'This is my beloved Son. My favor rests on him.' " (Matthew 3:16–17.)

Enshrined in the place of highest esteem, on an Everest of Glory, is the man for all ages: Jesus Christ. His life dominates the human scene from the dawn of Genesis until the end of time.

—Jeane Dixon

5. The Call to Glory

GLORY!!
WHAT IS GLORY, ANYWAY?

The dictionary defines *glory* literally as "praise, honor, or distinction, accorded by common consent."

But I speak of the greater glory—the Glory of God! The glory which is so shining, so resplendent, so dazzling in brilliance, that it lights the universe!

Of course, there are degrees of glory, from the faintest of praise to the greatest of ticker-tape parades. There is the ephemeral glory of public acclaim which quickly fades, and the immortal glory of men who have shaped the story of man: Caesar, Einstein, Churchill, and Saint George. Outshining even them are all the religious leaders who have told men by word and example how to live in peace and fellowship with other men and thus honor the reign of God.

In the place of highest esteem, enshrined in an Everest of glory, is the Man of All Ages: Jesus Christ. His life governs the human scene from the dawn of Genesis till the end of time.

Will the human drama of life on earth be exported to other worlds for endless ages, like special casts taking a hit show on the road, when space travel becomes feasible? Or will it be totally snuffed out, as described in

Chapter Twenty-four of Saint Matthew, as our little ball of earth goes spiraling back into the sun, from whence it came? Is the earth essentially a grave, a cradle, a test tube, or an incubator?

I believe the whole of it is a work of art.

I believe the creation of living man is the masterpiece of God. I believe that we live in the Bethlehem of the universe, that is to say, wherever we live there also lives Jesus in our hearts—if we but accept Him. This is not to restrict the Spirit of Christ to our own limited knowledge of the Incarnation. The power and goodness of God are not limited to our own world. It is to say that the same Power which creates life and worlds is the energizing force behind the intelligence and will which drive us forth to seek new worlds to inhabit.

No one knows just yet what waits to be discovered on those little islands in the suns of other constellations or whether we shall acclaim future Columbuses who will come back and tell us. Nor are we able to speculate on limits to the Incarnation of God's glory beyond the feeble potencies of our human eyes and minds.

For the secret of peace in any life is the choice of the spirit that spoke through Jesus telling men and women to sublimate their differences through love of God and neighbor. How simple it would be if only people lived by the Golden Rule: Do to others as you would have them do to you. The refrain of Bethlehem, the key to survival and well-being, is the same as it always was: Peace through goodwill! The old idea of justice—an eye for an eye—is no longer applicable. Something more is needed now: action upon the principle of love.

The valley of the Fertile Crescent, which arcs across the northern part of the Syrian desert, is not only the cradle of Western civilization; it is likewise the Bethlehem of the spirit. It was the lush beauty and fertility of the Tigris and Euphrates Valley that gave form and substance to the Eden epics from Gilgamesh to Genesis.

The Hebrew scribes differed always from the others in writing from a religious motivation—in this case, explaining the nature of man and his fall from grace.

It was from the same locale that Indo-European culture crept north and west, giving birth to the Latin language—mother of European tongues—and Greek, the other parent of Mediterranean culture. It was from the Tigris and Euphrates Delta that Abraham began his journey from Ur to the Promised Land. It was in the same human heartland that David sang, Solomon reigned, the prophets raged, and Christ was born. The biblical Journeying, the Crucifixion, the Resurrection, nearly all took place in the Crescent. Resplendent with age and tradition, it will be the scene of yet more prophetic fulfillment, bloodshed, and tragic warring before man's final reconciliation with our God.

It is hard to imagine what the Jordan Valley was like in biblical days. Visiting the Holy Land today, one sees not only the bleak, barren hills, denuded of nearly all trees and verdure, but a land that once thrilled the dying Moses and was described by Hebrew scouts as "flowing with milk and honey." The gently rolling hills and plains were once covered with vineyards, orchards, olive groves, and seas of waving grain. There was some grazing by sheep and goats, which would multiply over the centuries and shear much of the land of its verdure, turning it into the semi-desert we see today.

Moses was to view the Jordan Valley from the heights of Mount Pisgah in one of the cruel ironies of all time. Having led his people out of their bondage in Egypt and forged them into a nation during the forty years of wandering in the Sinai Desert, they were ready to cross the last frontier and take the Promised Land from a people sunk in a morass of vice and infidelity. "Ah, let me cross over," Moses pleads in Chapter Three of Deuteronomy, "and see this good land beyond the Jordan, this fine hill country." (Deuteronomy 3:25.)

But the plan of God was otherwise. Like Jesus in Gethsemane, Moses was near the fulfillment of his earthly mission, and it was time to pass on. " 'Enough!' the Lord said to me. 'Speak to me no more of this. Go up to the top of Pisgah and look out to the west, and to the north, and to the south, and to the east. Look well, for you shall not cross this Jordan.' " (Deuteronomy 3: 26-27.)

So Moses commissioned Joshua to lead the people into Canaan; then he died there on the mountain. The Israelites prospered in Canaan, as God had promised Abraham. The epochal feats of Joshua crumbling the walls at Jericho; David slaying Goliath; Samson demolishing the temple of the Philistines; Elijah destroying the golden idol of Baal; the stories of Judith, Ruth, Esther, and the Maccabees give way to the gentler coming of the Prince of Peace, of whom it was said: "A bruised reed he shall not break, and a smoldering wick he shall not quench" (Isaiah 42:3).

A thousand years after King David's brilliant reign the valley was still green and beautiful. Like the legendary Sweet Afton, the Jordan flowed gently on. John, called "the Baptizer," now entered the scene. Reintroducing an ancient rite of purification, he established himself as an institution on the banks of the holy river. From all Israel the crowds flocked out to hear John preach and to be baptized.

In the tradition of the older prophets, the words of John the Baptizer were harsh and fierce: "You brood of vipers!" he exploded, the fire of God fuming forth. "Who told you to flee from the wrath to come?

"Give some evidence that you mean to reform. Do not begin by saying to yourselves, 'Abraham is our Father.' I tell you, God can raise up children to Abraham from these stones. Even now the ax is laid to the root of the tree. Every tree that is not fruitful will be cut down and thrown into the fire." (Luke 3:7-9.)

It was the same John, in a calmer mood, however, who anticipated Jesus immediately after another such outburst: "Let the man with two coats give to him who has none. The man who has food should do the same." (Luke 3:11.)

To the Roman soldiers of occupation he said: "Don't bully anyone. Denounce no one falsely. Be content with your pay." (Luke 3:14.)

One day, thigh-deep in the river, John had just completed a baptism when he glanced up at the people awaiting their turn on the bank. Among them was the imposing figure of a man about his own age. The Baptizer addressed Him in words that have occasioned wonder and mystery ever since. "I should be baptized by you, yet you come to me!" (Matthew 3:14.)

How had John recognized the Messiah?

For centuries this question engaged theologians and there were many theories, some highly controverted. They ranged all the way from prenatal recall (Freud was not the first to perceive such a phenomenon), to elaborate visions and revelations. Like scientists and sociologists, theologians often must explain everything in terms of their own theories to give them any credence.

My own solution to the "mystery" is much simpler. John was psychic.

Being psychic myself, I can easily understand the divine inspiration.

As thousands know from direct experience, and millions indirectly through the published word, I have been able to know with certainty a whole network of things about people just by making contact with them and also to tell a good many others certain things about relatives and friends whom I have never met. It is simply a talent, one more common than generally believed. Like a gift of painting or music, it can be more fully developed, though it seldom is.

John the Baptizer also had the gift of prophecy, and it

enabled him to recognize Jesus beyond the shadow of any doubt.

The extrasensory perception, by which one is able to pick up what we term *vibrations*, is entirely distinct and apart from a revelation of some great event of historic significance, such as the coming of Christ or the assassination of President Kennedy. John the Baptist had both gifts; one enabled him to recognize Jesus on the banks of the Jordan when meeting Him for the first time; the other was the source of his proclamation to the Pharisees and Sadducees: "I baptize you in water for the sake of reform, but the one who will follow me is more powerful than I. I am not even fit to carry his sandals. He it is who will baptize you in the Holy Spirit and fire." (Matthew 3:11.)

At first John did not fully recognize Jesus, and the complete significance of His identity dawned slowly. For he says in Chapter One of Saint John's Gospel: "I confess I did not recognize him, though the very reason I came baptizing with water was that he might be revealed to Israel." (John 1:31.)

This I can appreciate also, for with even the most gifted psychics, the full potential of a truly great personality does not dawn all at once, but comes up in the consciousness slowly, like the longest day of the year. Thus it was with John and Jesus, for the same gospel tells of the Baptizer's pointing out Jesus to his followers as the "Lamb of God"—"Look! There is the Lamb of God who takes away the sin of the world!" (John 1:29.)

This reference was to the rite of the Passover; the symbolism was to Christ as the sacrificial lamb of Calvary, acting out the redemptive drama. After pointing out Jesus, John continues: "It is he of whom I said: 'After me is to come a man who ranks ahead of me, because he was before me.'" (John 1:30.)

Again John repeats that he did not immediately know Jesus, a curious trait which we find in both John and Jesus at moments of great crisis. But he resolves it by saying finally: "The one who sent me to baptize with water told me, 'When you see the Spirit descend and rest on someone, it is he who is to baptize with the Holy Spirit.' Now I have seen for myself and have testified, 'This is God's chosen One.'" (John 1:33-34.)

As the baptism ended and Jesus moved out of the water, John saw the "Spirit ... descend ... and hover over him" in the form of a dove, and there sounded in his ears the testimony of divinity: "This is my beloved Son. My favor rests on him." (Matthew 3:16-17.)

It was reflection upon this that gave John the Baptist all the certainty he needed and enabled him to say: "Now I have seen for myself and have testified, 'This is God's chosen One.'" (John 1:34.)

His "origin" as the prophet Micah said, "is from of old, from ancient times" (Micah 5:1); and Jesus Himself was to go even further, saying to Philip: "Whoever has seen me has seen the Father." (John 14:9.)

Jesus was about thirty years of age at the time of His baptism (Luke 3:23), the age for decisions of destiny in the lives of many great men. Little is known of Him from His twelfth year until He appears on the banks of the Jordan, insisting that John baptize Him. We hear of Him as He turned a teen-ager, in the temple of Jerusalem, where He so astonished the priests and doctors with His intelligence and wisdom at so young an age.

What of the lost years?

Although we know nothing of the details, we can assume that the young Jesus lived the life of the normal young Jew of His time. He carried water, tended a small garden, and learned to be a carpenter. He also learned to be literate and "search the Scriptures." That the family life of Joseph, Mary, and Jesus was a good one is evident from what happened on their trip to the temple when Jesus broke the surface of temple life with His brilliance at the temple school. His delicate sense of family discipline came out in the incident of His being "lost" and found by His parents, when He reminded them that He had a life of His own to live, to "be in my Father's house" (Luke 2:49). The generation gap, however, did not breach honor and respect, for He nevertheless "went down with them ... and came to Nazareth. and was obedient to them." (Luke 2:51.)

To be in His "Father's house," about His "Father's business" went back a long, long time, to the beginning of time. It began for His people with the call of Abraham we have already examined. It went on with the migration of the children of Abraham down into Egypt, where they grew into a people. It crescendoed again with the career of Moses, who led the people of Abraham out of Egypt and forged them into a nation. It ebbed and flowed in the Sinai Desert for forty years of pilgrimage to the "Promised Land." After the death of Moses it continued in the conquest of Canaan and the rise of the Jewish nation under David and Solomon to the pinnacle of its imperial power. The prophets took up God the Father's work and formed guard rails against the temptations of empire on one side and the decadence of idolatry on the other. Even more, they preserved hope in the coming Messiah as their people underwent the tortures of conquest and division, enslavement and occupation in their turn. The imperial forces of Assyria, Persia, Greece, and Rome rolled like seismic tides over the "chosen people," bringing heavy weather and good times, suffering and survival. As Jesus debated with the doctors and asked them unanswerable questions, the Romans were in control. Israel (or more properly speaking, Judah) had been occupied and "pacified" at least for a time. The life of Jesus was bracketed by those years. As He discoursed with the Rabbinic sages, all this must have been churning in His mind. It would be sorted out in His late teens and twenties as He neared the time of His own call, to take His own unique place in the history of mankind.

There is no "Life of Jesus" as such; all we have are the casual and fragmentary accounts of the Gospels, plus a few superficial references in Suetonius, Tacitus, Pliny the Younger, and Josephus. Even parts of the Gospels have been hotly disputed. But apart from all the controversy and challenge of the centuries, we now know enough, particularly in the perspective of history, to identify the Messiah and understand His message.

The salient facts of Jesus' life stand out like climactic acts in a classic drama. His birth is marked by extraordinary events that characterize His mission: there are the Wise Men, the Star of Bethlehem, King Herod, the Manger and the Shepherds, the Song of Angels, and the Virgin Mary. The little family flees the Herodian massacre directed at them, and after Herod's death they return. Then there is the long "hidden life" in Nazareth, the temple incident, a return to obscurity until Jesus breaks through the surface again with John the Baptist, after which it is clear that He went about for a time as a baptizer, not personally but through His disciples. Saint John's gospel tells us: "Later on, Jesus and his disciples came into Judean territory, and he spent some time with them there baptizing." (John 3:22) . . . "in fact, however, it was not Jesus himself who baptized, but his disciples." (John 4:2.) It has already been noted in Chapter Three that John the Baptizer moved the site of his operation upstream to "Aenon near Salim where water was plentiful." (John 3:23.)

John's greatest moment came at this point. "Rabbi," his disciples complained to him, "the man who was with you across the Jordan—the one about whom you have been testifying—is baptizing now, and everyone is flocking to him." (John 3:26.) John's hour had come! The greater had arrived and now the lesser must so acknowledge. We all face such a test at some point in maturity;

no one met it better than John. "You yourselves are witnesses to the fact that I said: 'I am not the Messiah: I am sent before him. . . . He must increase, while I must decrease.'" (John 3:28-30.)

A short time later John the Baptist was beheaded in prison, and Jesus said no greater man had ever lived (Matthew 11:11).

Between the time that Jesus was baptized by John and the time He began His own ministry of baptism He retired to the desert for five or six weeks of reflection and meditation. As He cut Himself off from all human communication to concentrate on the divine life, Jesus must have mused on the desert tradition that has made it the symbol of introspection and contemplation. It was in a deserted region that Abraham offered his sacrifice and received God's promise that "I will bless you abundantly and make your descendants as countless as the stars of the sky and the sands of the seashore." (Genesis 22:17.) It was in the same region that he spared the life of his son Isaac and thus ended for all time any approval of ritualistic human sacrifice in religion; that Jacob and his progeny went to Egypt to follow Joseph and begin the long formation of Israel as a people. It was out into the desert that Moses fled as a fugitive to tend the flocks of Jethro and there saw human destiny in the burning bush—ever consumed, but never spent. All Israel found God in the desert as a cloud by day and fire by night, giving them food and water and teaching them the awesome responsibilities of freedom and dependence upon God's providence. Elijah found God in the desert, the Essenes sought refuge there, and John the Baptist began his preaching in "the desert of Judea.'"

Jesus knew all this. He could not help recognizing that He was indeed the Messiah and that the testimony of John the Baptizer made it imperative to act.

Yet He was one thing more: He was free. He was tempted by Satan to relinquish his freedom, to become a great hero, a sensual hedonist, a celebrated wonder-worker. He was severely tempted, by a very real spirit of evil: destructive egotism, a brooding spirit of chaos that is the antithesis of peace and love, the spirit of self-centeredness—this is the "Devil" of which Scripture speaks.

It is not always easy to face the obligations of being human, as we know from reading about people witnessing others being murdered or the attitude we ourselves sometimes have toward people of other continents, races, or religious traditions. To be religious means much more than being human; it means, as Jesus taught, the effort toward perfecting our humanity without being self-righteous about it.

Jesus was like any normal man with all the normal drives in all things except sin (Hebrews 7:26). He loved the festive mood of a wedding, He was at home with the rich as well as the poor, He could become angry enough to wield the whip and drive hypocrites from the temple and sorrowful enough to weep over the death of Lazarus, His friend. He was kind to sinners and prostitutes; yet a man of unquestioned probity in His own life. He was remarkably free of the prejudices of His time, and He treated all men and women as equals.

He had gone about His "Father's business" so well that the Father was "well pleased." Yet now, as later in Gethsemane, He was tempted to ask that He be spared suffering and death! This is the real meaning of every temptation. In the desert of loneliness and isolation, faced with the cold of death and darkness, cast completely upon our own resources and God's providence, we meet our real selves—which is to say, our place in God's plan, both for us individually and in the overall scheme of things. We can either take it or not. Some of us, like Jesus, respond completely. Some of us are shocked by the alternatives and turn away from the deepest problems of the human condition, while others simply turn on their heels in rejection. Still more people have good intentions, but lose them in inconsistency and dreams. The majority seem to learn gradually over a long period of time that you cannot have your freedom and not use it. If you do not use it for something good it erodes with time, leaving a debris of aging promises of what might have been.

It takes most of us forty years to mature in the various deserts of life—or more. It took Jesus forty days.

As He trekked back to Galilee, Jesus knew that He had consented to do God's work.

HE HEEDED THE CALL TO GLORY!

"When they met again in Galilee, Jesus said to them, 'The Son of Man is going to be delivered into the hands of men who will put him to death, and he will be raised up on the third day.'" (Matthew 17:22-23.)

Jesus' examples of life, forgiveness, and brotherhood are the best guides for us all if we are to have hope for a brighter future—indeed, any future at all!

—Jeane Dixon

6. The Triple Threat

How do you measure the achievements of a life?

The life of Jesus of Nazareth is beyond measure. He dominates all human history like the figure of Christ the Redeemer which dominates the harbor of Rio de Janeiro. His is the life by which most of the world measures the passage of its allotted years in terms of before (B.C.) and after (A.D.) the birth of Christ.

Though He towers above us, He is still one of us, and therefore a consideration of the forces and circumstances which shaped His career will help us to understand the all-powerful influence of His life upon mankind.

A half-century before the birth of Jesus, the Roman Empire had expanded to the point where it took over the remnants of the old Alexandrian dominions, which included Palestine, an area about the size of the state of New Jersey. The Romans loved local collaborators; it made things so much easier! Never was anyone more suited to this role than an Arabian adventurer named Herod, a man who used the cruelest and most gruesome atrocities to gain his ends. Herod, who was not a Jew, sought Roman assistance to put himself in power in Palestine; he succeeded, but as one historian phrases it: "Herod invited the Romans in as friends; they remained as masters."

Under King Herod's rule of Israel a Jew could be

happier almost anywhere else than in Israel, for the conduct of this despot was so monstrous that it is difficult to believe. Even his friends and family lived in perpetual fear. Shortly after coming to power he had his brother-in-law murdered, then went on to execute his brother and his brother's wife. Against the advice of the Roman emperor, Augustus, he had his second wife's two sons executed upon their return from Rome, because their anger at their mother's death made them dangerous! A reign of terror marked by corruption, murder, and intrigue enabled Herod to remain in power for thirty-seven years. A liar himself, he made liars of others; himself corrupt, he bred corruption all about him; born a hater of man, he harvested such hate as had never before been seen in Israel.

Perhaps the worst of Herod's acts occurred when he was near death. Knowing how much the Jews detested him, and that they would rejoice to see him dead, he ordered a roundup of hundreds of the most important and respected figures in the kingdom, had them confined in an arena, and gave orders that all were to be killed immediately upon his death. "The Jews may not mourn for me," he said, "but they will mourn!" (Josephus Flavius.) Happily, Herod's sister was able to countermand the order when the king finally died.

Like all tyrants, Herod lived in constant fear of being assassinated or dethroned. As we know from the story of the Wise Men after the birth of Christ, this paranoiac fear of Herod's threatened the life of the newborn child Jesus for a time, and Mary and Joseph fled into Egypt with Him to escape the "slaughter of the innocents."*

---

* The death of King Herod in 4 B.C., after he had been absent from Jerusalem for some time, owing to illness, is an unquestioned historical fact. This circumstance and other data contained in the Gospel according to Luke 2:1-2 oblige us to assume that the birth of Our Lord occurred six or seven years previous to the date originally accepted in the Gregorian calendar, a fact now generally conceded by nearly all scholars.

After King Herod's death the kingdom was divided among three of his sons—Archelaus, Herod Antipas, and Philip—all half-brothers, for their father had many wives. Archelaus ruled Judea, Herod Antipas became ruler of Galilee and Perea, while Philip was given the northeastern section bordering Syria.

Archelaus is of interest to us because his many foolish acts led Rome to depose him, installing in his stead the first Roman governor of Judea, known as a procurator or imperial administrator. There were five of these during the lifetime of Jesus, the significant one being Pontius Pilate, who came to Jerusalem in 26 A.D. and continued to govern for ten years.

The son of Herod the Great whom we are interested in was Herod Antipas, who ruled in Jesus' home province, Galilee. A Roman lackey like his father, Antipas was scarcely more popular than his detested parent, for it is evident that he had inherited a goodly share of the old king's vicious tendencies. In Herod Antipas we meet the first of the three sinister influences which acted in concert, however unwittingly, to condemn Jesus of Nazareth to the Cross. The others were Roman power, in the person of Pontius Pilate, and a religious fanaticism embodied in the two great sects of Israel at that time—the Pharisees and the Sadducees. A Triple Threat to Our Lord!

Once He had begun to preach, Jesus was made continually aware of the displeasure of Herod Antipas, who had already beheaded John the Baptizer, and the activities of Jesus were therefore no more welcome than were those of John.

Finally, the situation got so tense that Our Lord fled northward, into Phoenicia, where He remained until the storm blew over. And then, shortly before that fatal last week, well-wishers informed Jesus that Herod Antipas had his intelligence agents out with orders to kill Him, whereupon Jesus declared: "Go tell that fox, 'Today and tomorrow I cast out devils and perform cures, and on the third day my purpose is accomplished. For all that, I must proceed on course today, tomorrow, and the day after, since no prophet can be allowed to die anywhere except in Jerusalem.' " (Luke 13:32-33.)

The guilt of Herod Antipas in the death of Jesus is obvious if one reads the Scriptures carefully. Chapter Twenty-three of Saint Luke tells the story, leaving no doubt that Herod Antipas, infamous son of an infamous father, could have saved Jesus when Pilate sent Him to Herod's court; but instead sent Him back to Pilate to be condemned.

"Pilate reported to the chief priests and the crowds, 'I do not find a case against this man.' But they insisted, 'He stirs up the people by his teaching throughout the whole of Judea, from Galilee, where he began, to this very place.' On hearing this Pilate asked if the man was a Galilean; and when he learned that he was under Herod's jurisdiction, he sent him to Herod, who also happened to be in Jerusalem at the time." (Luke 23:4-7.)

When Jesus appeared before Herod Antipas, the ruler questioned Him, but Jesus remained silent. Herod cynically asked to see a miracle performed, but Jesus rebuked the arrogant fox with uncompromising reserve. Meanwhile, priests and scribes stood by, shouting their accusations.

The Gospel according to Luke continues: "Herod and his guards then treated him with contempt and insult, after which they put a magnificent robe on him and sent him back to Pilate." (Luke 23:11.) This meant *to His death*.

What could Herod Antipas have done to save Jesus? He could have put Him under guard and had Him escorted back to Galilee to his own jurisdiction. That is obviously what Pilate hoped would happen. The Roman governor, as he said, could find no fault in Jesus, for he evidently disliked becoming involved in the religious dissensions of the Jews.

But there was a reason for Pilate's conciliatory gesture of sending Jesus to Herod. A year or two previously, Galileans attending Passover rites in Jerusalem had created a disturbance, and soldiers, ordered by Pilate, charged into the group and put many of them to death, much to Herod's displeasure.

Therefore, when Pilate saw a way to make amends by sending Jesus to Herod Antipas, he did so, thus effecting a reconciliation. "Herod and Pilate, who had previously been set against each other, became friends from that day," writes Saint Luke in Chapter 23:12.

The evil of the Herods was not to end with the death of Jesus, for eventually a grandson of the first Herod, named Herod Agrippa, came to rule in Judea after the ouster of Pilate, whose cruelties had caused so many disturbances that Rome thought it expedient to replace him with a local ruler. It was before Herod Agrippa that James the Apostle stood for judgment and was sentenced to death. Also before this Herod appeared Saint Paul, accused of heresy and subversion, but Paul's plea was so moving that Agrippa finally said in desperation, "A little more, Paul, and you will make a Christian out of me!" (Acts 26:28.)

It is difficult for us, living today, to comprehend the moral insensibility of the Roman Empire at that time.

The Gospels give very little idea of the actual state of political affairs in Israel, but it was a time of seething discontent, smoldering resentments, civil disturbances, and terrorist activity. There were periodic riots in the streets and mass executions. Rome had only one answer for rebellion—swift and unalterable retaliation.

The most desperate insurrection against Roman power occurred when Jesus was just a boy, but one may conclude that all His short life He must have remembered those days of bitterness. The revolt was led by a

Galilean named Judas (a very common name), and for a time it looked as though the great days of the Maccabees were to be repeated, with Israel once again freed of foreign domination. But the Romans sent reinforcements from Syria, and the dream of liberty was soon over—but not the revenge of Rome! The historian Josephus recounts that no less than *two thousand* of those who took part in the insurrection were crucified along the main roads of Judea and Galilee, while thousands more were sent into perpetual slavery, women and children included. What a terrible time it was!

Certainly from His earliest days Jesus must have been familiar with crucifixion—the atrocious form of execution that the merciless Romans devised—for such executions were happening all the time. Certainly on His journeys to Jerusalem for the Passover rites He must have witnessed time and time again figures hung on crosses along the route, their dying cries a warning to those who would challenge the power of Rome. This was the ominous threat which loomed unceasingly over the lives of all Jews, Jesus included.

Finally, Jesus Himself stood accused before the representative of Rome; it was Pontius Pilate who had the final say. However, an even greater reason for denunciation lies in the Roman Empire's defiling of the people, and surely this is a lesson for us today. As Rome ruled its subjects by terror and violence, they became infected with the same callousness in short order, for terror begets terror as violence begets violence. These very evils abound in our land today; are we likewise to become indifferent, to become hardened to injustice and cruelty?

Jesus, whose whole life had been one of kindness and forbearance, stood before His people, for whom He had done only good, and Pilate gave them a choice. Not between Jesus and Barabbas, for that was already decided, but "What am I to do with Jesus, the so-called Messiah?" And then all the malevolence of Roman rule reaped its harvest of hatred. "Crucify him!" they shouted, and Pilate, functionary of Rome, whose policy was not to meddle unnecessarily in the religious affairs of his Jewish subjects, sacrificed our Lord on the altar of political expediency (Matthew 27:22).

We have accounted for two of the three factors which led to the Crucifixion of our Lord. There remain the two principal sects then active among the people. Though Jesus was harassed continually during His ministry by the Pharisees, it was a Sadducee, the high priest Caiaphas, who delivered Him to Pilate for execution. Thus, Sadducees definitely played a part in the final betrayal.

There were, however, two lesser sects in the ancient land of the Jews during this period, the Zealots and the Essenes. These are of interest to us because of their *indirect* involvement in the ministry of Jesus. The Man from Galilee had little use for either group, a disapproval which shows up unmistakably in His teaching. Essene rigidity, their fasting, their isolation from women, their obsession with the Law, Jesus could not accept; for Our Savior taught that man was meant to be happy, not a slave to marital and social austerity, but a beneficiary of their blessings. God's blessings are meant to be enjoyed. Everywhere Jesus appeared He brought love and tenderness, understanding and lightness of heart. Too many have made religion joyless and somber—*Jesus did not!*

The Zealots were entirely another people. These are "the violent men" Jesus unquestionably had in mind when he spoke of "violent men seizing the Kingdom of God." Zealots differed from the three other groups in their impassioned and fanatical opposition to foreign domination. They were the guerrillas of their day, adept at all the sinister arts of terrorism. They struck mainly in darkness, slaying, burning, and destroying. What made them especially annoying to the Romans and their collaborators alike was their complete lack of regard for their own personal safety. Josephus describes this characteristic of the Zealots: "They have an inviolable attachment to liberty, and say that only God is their Ruler and Lord. They do not fear any kind of death, nor indeed do they heed the deaths of their relatives and friends."

Attempts have been made to link Jesus of Nazareth with the Zealots, based mainly on the fact that Simon the Zealot was one of His disciples, but this is absurd. Simon was undoubtedly a Zealot, who gave up terrorism and violence when he became one of our Lord's apostles. And how erroneous to assume that the triumphant entry into Jerusalem on Palm Sunday was meant as a gathering of the forces of insurrection! An insurgent bent on conquest does not enter Jerusalem riding a donkey, surrounded by simple country folk waving palm branches and shouting hosannas. He comes armed, men-at-arms with him! Pontius Pilate, the supposedly well-informed Roman governor with agents all over, had no previous knowledge whatever of Jesus when He was brought before him. Some spy network that was!

By no stretch of the imagination was Jesus a man of violence, although He had his moments of righteous anger too. Our Savior was preeminently a Man of Peace. Remember how He kept John and James from burning down a town when it refused to welcome them; how He told Peter he should forgive not seven times, but seventy times seven; how He reproved the apostles who wished to carry swords, warning that those who live by the sword perish by the sword; how He refused to stand by and see a woman stoned to death? The One who would turn the other cheek if struck would deem the death of a lone Roman sentry at the hands of a Zealot assassin as much an offense against God as any other death by violence, for Jesus understood that the Roman soldier was a prisoner of the system. Furthermore, Jesus foresaw correctly destruction for Israel occasioned by the activities of the Zealots and similar foes. In retaliation for terrorism and anarchy the Romans laid waste the land, utterly destroyed Jerusalem, and dispersed the Jews "before this generation passes."

But returning to the Pharisees, who were the main adversaries of Jesus, these people saw the Nazarene preacher as a clear and present danger to their entrenched position as arbiters of the Law. What flaws and fallacies Jesus saw in their practices! Just like us today, they strained at the gnat and swallowed the camel. Their system was both complex and artificial, providing little solace for the mass of Jews, but so great was their power that to cross them could be fatal. In charge of interpreting the Law were the famous "scribes," whom Jesus castigated on numerous occasions. They were in essence lawyers who had developed such a mass of rules and traditions surrounding the practice of Judaism that ordinary Jews, though bound by these rules, found it too difficult to apply them to their simple lives.

The Sadducees were the Brahmans of the Jews, the highest clerical caste, and differed from the Pharisees in several important beliefs, mainly that of an afterlife. This group was most active in Judea, particularly Jerusalem, where they held high priestly positions, collaborated continually with the Roman rulers, and prided themselves on their wealth and aristocracy. One might say that while the Pharisees were the legislators of Judaism, the Sadducees were its executives and the scribes its judiciary.

Prior to His final week, the Sadducees had given Jesus little trouble, but in Jerusalem He moved in Sadducean territory. Reports quickly reached the high priest Caiaphas in regard to the fracas in the temple court between Jesus and the money changers. Caiaphas' alarm can be imagined, for money changing was a profitable business. He also learned of the "blasphemous" oratory of the Galilean Preacher, stirring up the crowds in an occupied country. His dismay grew. But what irked the Sadducees most about Jesus was His insistence upon an afterlife in eternity, a Kingdom of Heaven, in which they had no faith.

Agents of the high priest were sent out to bait Jesus with loaded questions, such as the one about the wife who had seven husbands, whether or not it was permissible to pay taxes to the Roman occupying power, and the penalty for the woman taken in adultery.

We may only conclude that the Crucifixion of Jesus came about through these three immediate forces working in concert. Herod Antipas, insensate son of a monstrous father; Pontius Pilate, who found no fault in Jesus but sacrificed Him for political reasons; and the religious fanatics of the time who wanted Him done away with for all time so as to preserve their archaic, sterile system.

They were all light-years behind Jesus; His common sense, His overriding compassion and profound wisdom in meeting human problems with the universal insight of God was beyond their ability to understand. His everlasting testimony to His own divinity was His famous, final prayer: "Father, forgive them; they do not know what they are doing." (Luke 23:34.)

Today religion faces the same blind spiritual forces. Roman power symbolizes the "omnipotent state," which decrees or denies religious freedom and how it shall or shall not be exercised. It is the archetype of totalitarian repression, which acknowledges no power but its own. The Zealots were like the extremists of right-wing groups, modeled on some past ideal, who made their bid for total power in tightly knit bands on some all-or-nothing power play.

Pontius Pilate lives on in the liberal cultists, the Consciousness II people, who believe that somehow by expediency and political tact we can make "progress" work for everybody. But as a matter of fact, it never works for everybody. Then the Consciousness III people come along, and, though less lucid and eloquent, they come to the same conclusion: that things are all ending in a hopeless mess, beyond redemption. So they resist with understandable and inactive anarchy by simply refusing to go along with the mess; that is, passively resisting the Establishment.

If we are to save our world as a free, safe, and agreeable place in which to live, we need to begin with the love of God and obey His Commandments—never forget that there are ten of them—for anything less than that will lead us into the same kind of destruction that ended the Roman Empire.

Jesus said: "I came that they might have life and have it to the full." (John 10:10.) His examples of love, forgiveness, and brotherhood are the best guides we have for the common effort which must be made by all of us without exception, if we are to have any hope for a brighter future—indeed, any future at all!

The signs are upon us, and ominous beyond description! Take heed!

"Seek first his kingship over you, his way of holiness, and all these things will be given you besides." (Matthew 6:33.)

The golden voice of Jesus will not be silenced. We have a great opportunity to hear it again. It is vital that we heed it!

—Jeane Dixon

7. The Golden Voice of Jesus

Why was Jesus of Nazareth crucified?

"He stirs up the people by his teaching" (Luke 23:5), said the chief priests to Pontius Pilate. The Roman governor, fearing a riot, sanctioned the sentence of death.

A day or two before, the authorities had sent out agents to seize Jesus as He preached, but the agents returned empty-handed. "Some of them even wanted to apprehend him. However, no one laid hands on him. When the temple guards came back, the chief priests and Pharisees asked them: 'Why did you not bring him in?' 'No man ever spoke like that before,' the guards replied." (John 7:44-46.)

Decidedly, this Man who could sway crowds with such ease was, in view of the meaning of His message, a threat to the Establishment, an alarming adversary of the *status quo*. His condemnation of entrenched power had implications they could not allow to stand. H.G. Wells, in his perceptive commentary on the life of Jesus in *Outline of History*, speaks of this: "Perhaps the priests and rulers and the rich men understood Him better than His followers." Quite true. His followers heard compassion and hope in His words; those who sat in the seats of authority heard only a threat to a way of life they did not want to give up.

To the forsaken and dejected, Jesus preached hope; to the slaves His words brought spiritual self-respect; to the weak His words gave strength of soul; to the poor His words gave personal dignity. There is no distinction of persons in the Kingdom of God except for distinguishing between those who use the gifts He gave them, and those who do not (Matthew 23:19-23).

He does no less for all of us today.

Though opposition to Jesus had been building up for months, one specific speech sealed His doom. This was the violent condemnation He delivered during that last week in Jerusalem. It was not a long speech, but He condemned in justifiable anger intolerance, hypocrisy, and entrenched privilege. After this public censure, the chief priests had but one thought: Get rid of Him!

How true even today! Intolerance, hypocrisy, and entrenched privilege sought to kill Jesus; in 1971 they say "God is dead."

Note Chapter Twenty-three of Saint Matthew:

"Woe to your scribes and Pharisees, you frauds! You shut the doors of the kingdom of God in men's faces, neither entering yourselves nor admitting those who are trying to enter.

"Woe to you scribes and Pharisees, you frauds! You travel over sea and land to make a single convert, but once he is converted you make a devil of him twice as wicked as yourselves. . . .

"Woe to you scribes and Pharisees, you frauds! You pay tithes on mint and herbs and seeds while neglecting the weightier matters of the law, justice and mercy and good faith . . . Blind guides! You strain out the gnat and swallow the camel!"

"Woe to you scribes and Pharisees, you frauds! You cleanse the outside of a cup and dish, and leave the inside filled with loot and lust! . . .

"Woe to you scribes and Pharisees, you frauds! You are like the whitewashed tombs, beautiful to look at on

the outside but inside full of filth and dead mens' bones. Thus you present to view a holy exterior while hypocrisy and evil fill you within.

"Woe to you scribes and Pharisees, you frauds! You erect tombs for the prophets and decorate the monuments of the saints. You say, 'Had we lived in our forefathers' time we would not have joined them in shedding the prophets' blood.' Thus you show that you are the sons of the prophets' murderers. Now it is your turn; fill up the vessel measured out by your forefathers. Vipers' nest! Brood of serpents! How can you escape condemnation to Gehenna?" (Matthew 12:13-33.)

Reading this speech, one wonders: Where is the *gentle Jesus* of other Scripture passages, the Good Shepherd spreading sweetness and light? We see no cheek turning in this outburst of righteous anger, no offer of clemency. God is willing to forgive, and there is redemption for all through Jesus, but one must meet the Lord on His terms.

Like Nathan, who braved the wrath of a king to condemn his wantonness—"Why have you spurned the Lord and done evil in his sight?" (2 Samuel 12:9)—Jesus braved the wrath of the entire Establishment of His day, an act that finally cost Him His life. Pontius Pilate may have found no fault in Jesus, but the scribes and Pharisees and the chief priests did—they felt He was too outspoken!

Now let us go back in time to another speech, a speech that contained no anger, condemned no one, but instead preached love and kindness, faith and goodness. It was a speech which may have seemed innocuous to the enemies of Jesus, but was in reality a *far greater threat* than the speech in Jerusalem.

The Sermon on the Mount was the supreme discourse of Jesus, the cornerstone of Christian ethics. It is the voice of conscience, a moment of tenderness in a harsh world, a poem that links man to God and justifies our right to live serenely in God's grace. It holds up a mirror to man's confusions, calms his anxieties, and allows his aspirations to soar. It shames the philosophers and poets —the former because its insight towers high above their tedious abstractions; the latter because, like the happy face of a child, the sermon is more beautiful in its simplicity than all their studied elegance.

Through a few phrases of Jesus' Sermon on the Mount He lifts men above themselves, transcending their human nature and transporting them to His Father's perfect world of grace and friendship.

"After he had sat down his disciples gathered around him, and he began to teach them:

'How blest are the poor in spirit: the reign of God is theirs.

Blest too are the sorrowing; they shall be consoled.

Blest are the lowly; they shall inherit the land.

Blest are they who hunger and thirst for holiness; they shall have their fill.

Blest are they who show mercy; mercy shall be theirs.

Blest are the single-hearted for they shall see God.

Blest too the peacemakers; they shall be called sons of God.

Blest are those persecuted for holiness' sake; the reign of God is theirs.

Blest are you when they insult you and persecute you and utter every kind of slander against you because of me.'" (Matthew 5:1-11.)

These are the words which finally brought the Roman Empire to its knees. The despots could flay, burn, and crucify, but they were helpless against the weapon Jesus had placed in the hands of men, the power of God's love. Over three centuries later, Julian the Apostate, last Roman emperor to try to turn back the clock, to stem the surging ground swell of Christianity, was to die with a tribute to the Beatitudes on his lips: "You have conquered, O Galilean!"

Jesus followed the Beatitudes with injunctions as to

how people should conduct their lives, in clear language, which no one could possibly misunderstand. Strewn throughout the discourse are phrases familiar to all of us, for they are part of our Christian heritage (Matthew 5, 6, 7):

". . . salt of the earth."

". . . a lamp . . . under a bushel . . ."

"No man can serve two masters. . . . You cannot give yourself to God and money."

"Enough, then, of worrying about tomorrow. Let tomorrow take care of itself. Today has troubles enough of its own."

"If you want to avoid judgment, stop passing judgment."

"Do not . . . toss your pearls before swine."

"But how narrow is the gate that leads to life, how rough the road . . ."

"False prophets . . . come . . . in sheep's clothing but underneath are wolves on the prowl. You will know them by their deeds."

During the course of the sermon, Jesus gave to the assembled multitude the simplest and yet most perfect of all invocations to the heavenly Father, the Lord's Prayer, prefacing it with a brief comment on what He thought was wrong with "showoff" piety: "Pray to your Father in private." (Matthew 6:6.)

As He came to the end, He said: "Anyone who hears my words and puts them into practice is like the wise man who built his house on rock. When the rainy season set in, the torrents came and the winds blew and buffeted his house. It did not collapse; it had been solidly set on rock. Anyone who hears my words but does not put them into practice is like the foolish man who built his house on sandy ground. The rains fell, the torrents came, the winds blew and lashed against his house. It collapsed under all this and was completely ruined.

"Jesus finished this discourse and left the crowds spellbound at his teaching. The reason was that he taught with authority and not like their scribes." (Matthew 7:24-29.)

The speech in Jerusalem and the Sermon on the Mount were two outstanding discourses, but the golden voice of Jesus was speaking all the time, sometimes to a handful of people, but more frequently, as His renown grew, to immense crowds.

But Jesus had another vocal talent, a skill at debate, which was equally impressive. His adversaries, some of them highly trained in dialectics, often attempted to lure Him into a trap, to no avail.

"Is it lawful to pay tax to the emperor or not?" they asked, hoping to trick Him into treason. "Give to Caesar what is Caesar's, but give to God what is God's," was the swift answer (Matthew 22:17, 21).

They accused Him of doing Satan's work when He cast out devils on the Sabbath, whereupon Jesus made his devastating reply: "A town or household split into factions cannot last for long. If Satan is expelling Satan, he must be torn by dissension. How, then, can his dominion last?" (Matthew 12:25-26.)

One of God's divine gifts to His incarnate Son was a golden voice. He used it to thwart His opponents, to castigate the evil and unjust, to soothe the disturbed, to heal the sick and maimed, and also to censure hypocrisy. He used it to develop and instruct apostles, who would carry His message to the far corners of the earth; to comfort the wretched; and lastly, He used it to spread universal love, to give even the lowliest existence a preview of heaven and a promise of immortality.

In America some are trying to silence the golden voice of Jesus. It began with the public schools where not even the name of God can now be legally mentioned! There are only two other governments in the world that can match this usurping of an inherent God-given right: Communist China and the Soviet Union. In those nations liberty was a casualty of social progress—what little they had—in the United States our precious freedom can vanish the same way. Already we are so preoccupied with civil liberties that we have forgotten the deeper *religious liberties* from which they originally sprang. Because dissenters and fanatics abused their rights and ours, are we to reply by curtailing the rights of all!?! It is as if we sought to correct embezzlement by abolishing money! We could more easily do without a medium of exchange than without a standard of religious ethics.

The state of our educational system and the condition of our youth should be enough to demonstrate the fallacy. As religion has declined and morality waned, juvenile crime and drug abuse have soared beyond control. As if that were not bad enough, the quality of education in all but our best schools is the subject of near despair in every educational forum. The dilemmas are always blamed on lack of funds; but the debaters always forget that there was better education when there was less money. Have we grown so blind that we cannot see the correlation of all these factors now corroding our society? Can we honestly believe that our mobile, rootless, amoral youth culture is unrelated to the steady deterioration of religious faith, discipline, and morals? Are we willing just to shrug it off and surrender to the immoralities, drugs, and rootlessness?

Youth are not the only sufferers, of course, but we too must bear the burden of facing an apocalyptic future for which we have failed to prepare not only our youth but ourselves as well.

Lieutenant Calley has one point in common with the hapless Vietnamese who died at My Lai, an ironic, contrived martyrdom: he was first de-Christianized, then de-humanized, and finally held individually to account for the inevitable consequences of all involved.

Instead of seeking first the reign of God and His justice, we first seek out evils in religious organizations and then condemn them. It is not enough simply to denounce or expose evils; it is even more necessary, as Saint Paul said, to overcome evil by doing good. There is no shortage of slanderers and detractors in the land, but there is a famine of the word of God, of truth, and of love.

We have memorized the evils of a religious past, the inquisitions, wars, and burning of saints. We congratulate ourselves that since we have exorcised the spirits of another age, such evils cannot plague us here and now.

But they are happening here and now!

With the advent of Social Security, the income tax, extensive Government regulation of business, industry, and finance, the draft, licenses of all kinds, and insurance laws came the basic tools of social control. Augmented by computer banks, Government files, and an army of electronic snoopers, there are already in existence the means for our opposing forces to take over American society. If we do not develop the spiritual fiber to get control of this monster it will make the prophecies of horror come true before 1984.

I foresee basic changes in American life by the end of this century that will completely alter our way of life. The present deterioration of dignity and self-respect will lead us steadily downhill in crime, sin, and immorality until the outbreak of war—serious global war—will bring us to our senses.

The two-party political system will vanish from the national scene, and there will be repressive measures taken, the like of which we find unbelievable now. Lack of a workable foreign policy will contribute to this. The lack of vision of our national leaders in government, labor unions, and business and professional organizations will all help to bring this about. It will be the result, so to speak, of blindness to political, economic, social, and international forces. The blame, of course, will not rest entirely with us; but it will weigh more heavily upon us because, of all the peoples of the world, we should take the responsibilities of leadership most seriously. This is our heritage.

However, the voice of God will not be silenced, in public, in church, or in the classroom. "God can raise up children to Abraham from these very stones." (Matthew 3:9.)

Even my own small voice has not been stilled, though it has been threatened! A ghostly shade with an evil mask asks if perhaps my prophecies could not have brought about assassinations, crises of confidence, and "possible danger." As if I were to blame for it all! He wonders if it would be "violating any of the canons of free speech" to outlaw me.

Should I not warn my country and its principals of fatal dangers that in the past have proved only too real and imminent? If I tell someone to drive carefully, does that make me "by the power of suggestion" responsible for his or her next automobile mishap? No, it does not.

For people who profess not to believe in me or in my prophecies, they certainly go to great lengths to contrive reasons for my being silenced. These reasons are like all the warped, illogical ones that were produced to outlaw prayer and reading of the Bible in public schools.

For that matter valid reasons were found for believing Hitler by those who wanted to believe in him, for dumping nuclear wastes into the ocean, and even for crucifying Christ.

No doubt some very intelligent people had, what were

to them at least, valid reasons why we should go to war in Indochina, why Caesar should be assassinated, and why the Hebrew prophets should be stoned. Sadly, we find it easy enough to rationalize the manipulation of our religious faith, the persecution of minorities, and the contamination of international relations almost beyond endurance.

Now we are dredging up reasons for polluting our minds and souls as well. While we legalize every kind of printed abomination, we would outlaw our prophets and visionaries.

Well did Isaiah prophesy of you, hypocrites!

While some publications spew enough poison to sicken a city, the warnings of God are repressed by them.

The golden voice of Jesus will not be silenced. It is vital that we heed it.

Lyubov Bershadskaya described again this year what life is like in a country that banishes God and lives by reason. She spent years in Soviet prisons, principally because she is a Jew. Recently she was permitted to emigrate to Israel. Then it all came out. Her lurid accounts of persecution take one back to the horror camps of World War II. There were no ovens in Russia or Siberia, but there was enslavement. Protest brought reprisals where "tanks smashed into the crowd, directly into living flesh, grinding people up." Hundreds of people died in that Red hell, and many more lost their minds.

The principles of religious faith and love of God are the only remedies for "man's inhumanity to man"; the principles have to be real and thoroughgoing, not just nominal. We once had that unity of faith in our pioneers, but we have been losing it progressively in each generation until the trend has fragmented us. A new and dangerous aggressiveness is straining the social bond to its elastic limit. The spirit of altruism, love, and goodwill that is its antidote does not come neatly packaged and handed to us; It comes only through our seeking God in a very personal way; it involves much prayer and meditation as well as many good works. The Church can be a great help, as it has been to many saints and scholars; or it can seem like the blind leading the blind, as it often does today, because of the evil forces purposely trying to destroy the organization of the Church.

Today we have a great opportunity to hear the golden voice of Jesus again. It bids us return to Jesus and His messages of eternal truth:

"I am the way, and the truth, and the life."

"Seek first his kingship over you, his way of holiness, and all these things will be given you besides."

"Give to Caesar what is Caesar's, but give to God what is God's."

"I give you a new commandment: Love one another. Such as my love has been for you, so must your love be for each other."

What a wonderful opportunity is ours to listen to this golden voice again!

And if we do not . . .

"He [the devil] brought death to man from the beginning, and has never based himself on truth; the truth is not in him. Lying speech is his native tongue; he is a liar and the father of lies." (John 8:44.)

The terrors of Hitler and Stalin cannot be explained in mere human terms. They are a sign of spiritual evil—yes—the devil himself!

—Jeane Dixon

8. What! The Devil?!

On the July Fourth 1971 holiday weekend, Naval Lieutenant Commander Rolland and his family celebrated Independence Day by viewing the fireworks display from the Washington Monument in Washington, D.C. Late in the evening he and his family headed for home. A man of many gifts, he was scheduled to leave for Vietnam before the month was over. His nineteen-year-old son, three younger children, and their friend were along, with Mrs. Rolland. The son, following in his father's footsteps, had a brilliant and promising future.

Commander Rolland was driving his family along Columbia Pike in Annandale, Virginia, when their station wagon was endangered by the tailgating of another car, primed for racing. As they approached Sleepy Hollow Road, there was the roar of supercharged power and the screech of broad-tread tires as the racing car swerved ahead of the station wagon and ground to a stop for the red light.

Another car pulled up behind the Rollands'. In anger, the lieutenant commander got out of his car and, in the dark of the late summer night, strode up to admonish the occupants of the car ahead. A bitter argument ensued. One or more of the occupants left the car and the harangue turned into a fight. The commander was knocked to the ground, and immediately his son left the station wagon to go to his rescue. One or more of the occupants of the car behind the Rollands' joined in the fight, turning it into a melee.

And then it happened.

Someone produced a gun. Into the tangle of people three shots were fired. One killed Commander Rolland, another killed his son. The other shot apparently went wild.

A scant few days later came the dual funeral for the victims and the arrests of the suspects. The whole woeful story was pieced together in the press.

Compare this tragic story with the story Jesus told of the Good Samaritan. Herein He told us to love our neighbor, to care for him, show him compassion, to do good even to those who hate and persecute us.

The Good Samaritan found a stranger who had been beaten and left for dead; he took him into town and paid for his recovery. In the murder of Commander Rolland and his son, exactly the opposite happened.

Why?

Surely it is not because Good Samaritans are so common or because their deeds are performed in confidence and classified Top Secret! Rather it is because the faith which inspired the love of the Good Samaritan has been waning for so many decades in human hearts it has now all but disappeared. Without the moorings of faith we have drifted so far in the easy currents of permissiveness and self-indulgence that the stronger tides of raw instinct are beginning to take over and the devil's influence is making itself felt more strongly than ever. The "tailgate murders" were the result of just such evil influence on people by the devil.

The same surrender to evil instincts kills and wounds more people on highways every year than does the overwhelming killing on the battlefields. As a form of human impatience this instinct is much more constant and subtle. Impatience is the first imperceptible movement toward anger, and it is when we are angry that the devil moves in and takes over, often resulting in tragedy.

The mildest offenders against intelligence and love, impatience and anger, cause most of the accidental deaths and suffering in the world every day. Impatience—not stupidity or malice—is basically the aggressive instinct which causes one to forge ahead faster than reason will allow. It leads to the anger that boils up against anything and anyone interfering with the will to advance. Finally, it can culminate in the murderous rage that follows when irrational anger is thwarted.

Commander Rolland's lack of patience, stemming from concern for his children's safety, brought his life to a tragic end. The murderous rage that led to the killings likewise brought disaster to his assailants.

Such needless suffering! And all for what?

I once had a vision of crowds of people walking over the tops of buildings in Washington, trampling down the authority of society and its government. I said at the time that this is not the way to achieve justice for individuals or minority groups or anyone as far as that is concerned. Every individual and every group constituting the larger society must earn a place in that society and cooperate in its growth and development. If they try to bring legitimate government to a standstill or force it to conform to their ideas, they bring about the same reversion to force and instinct that polarizes people into attitudes of injustice and war.

We must not forge ahead angrily over those who oppose us! We do not prove our superiority over others by force, but by love, work, tolerance, and generosity. This is the difference between the Good Samaritan system of a free society and the "tailgate murders" syndrome that sets in when we fail the test of patience, tolerance, and love.

God is author of the one, the devil the instigator of the other.

What! The devil?!

"Can you be serious?" people ask. "Surely you're not going to blame most of the trouble in the world on the devil! Not today. . . ."

When I reply that there is no other way of accounting for drug addiction, alcoholism, crime, newspaper sensationalism, and so on, they stop smiling. These are no laughing matters. Evil never is.

I often counter their incredulous questions with others: why so much evil in an otherwise good and beautiful world? How can you account for war, crime, prisons, riots, racial hatreds, and all the other lamentable consequences of ill will in human history? Why is the suicide rate higher in the most progressive and seemingly "enlightened" countries. Why are some of our most brilliant and capable citizens addicted to alcoholism? Why do revolutionaries turn around and themselves do the very same things they rebel against? Why do we not learn from the incredible sum total of human sorrow and suffering in history, and profit thereby?

These are staggering questions.

In 1918, when World War I ended, the generals and politicos gathered around the conference table at Versailles and worked out a peace treaty of sorts. They represented the best talents the nations had to offer at that particular time, but there was no vision, spiritual or otherwise, and now the whole tragic scenario of the century has to be rewritten.

After World War II the architects of peace did a little better job, but still have not met the needs of one world under God!

We might address a very reasonable question to the psychologists of our time. Why couldn't the treaties and agreements, good or bad, be carried out without wars intervening? Is it because we have not yet suffered enough or learned enough from our suffering, to step finally and completely over the threshold of lasting peace?

Answers range from the politics of Hitlerian Europe to the nature of man himself. I say they all miss the point of the question, which is a religious one. Religious answers must be forthcoming after much deeper thought.

The peace treaty of 1945 was a great improvement over that of 1918, so perhaps we did learn a little. Owing mostly to American influence, it was for the most part a forgiving and generous covenant. Victors and vanquished alike prospered, so that former enemies became energetic competitors in the postwar period, a development unprecedented in history.

But the same ancient mischief is afoot at a much deeper point of psychological motivation and moral judgement. Old forces in new contexts on a vast scale are again maneuvering for mastery of the human spirit. The conflict is now truly global, the stakes total. England, France, and Germany have bit parts in the recurring and terrible drama of another world war, one to be unprecedented in violence and suffering by all those gone before. Russia, China, and the United States have taken over the leading roles. It will be utterly fantastic and annihilating—like nothing we have ever known.

It could be prevented!

We might ask our simple but profound question a third time: why not avoid such a war? Why not achieve world peace and progress peacefully, through the already existing machinery?

Why not, indeed?

The question is not naive, simplistic, or flippant. It is, as I have said, a matter of steadfast religious faith. And because much of the world is officially irreligious, it follows that it is unable to deal effectively with problems essentially religious in nature.

It will not always be so. Peace, well-being, demographic control are all attainable ideals, which will be realized in the next century; but in the present state of conventional wisdom and spiritual poverty they certainly will be difficult to achieve in this one.

The Strategic Arms Limitation Talks conferees took a whole year to accomplish little—likewise, representatives at the Paris Peace Talks play-acted out their little farce while men died daily in Southeast Asia. The Common Market Nations agonized for years over contentions such as those settled in America during the early summer of 1776 in a few short weeks, while George Washington pleaded with a laggard Continental Congress from an uncertain battlefield and the British Fleet lay at the ready off Long Island.

Nations and statesmen can do the impossible, but only, it seems, when an enemy waits just outside the gates. Fear seems to be the condition of progress. Men simply cannot agree to disarm or preserve the environment without some critical urgency.

Tell me why!

Let me answer the enigma in the only way it can be answered: the mills of God grind slowly, but they grind exceedingly fine. Or, in the terminology of an older theology: "Unless the Lord build the house, they labor in vain who build it." (Psalms 127:1.)

The Lord is always at work in human affairs. In us, He is building the human society of the future, already discernible in its broadest degree; and this is what human history is all about.

There is also an opposing and negative force at work, a destructive spirit that fouls up lives and conferences in seeking to undo the work of God, and that is what this is all about.

The interplay of these creative and destructive powers is the thesis and antithesis of Marx's dialectic, the yin and the yang of oriental thought, the God and Satan of biblical theology. One is the truth of reality, the other, the delusion of distorted intellect. The former is the principle of life and growth, the latter of decline and death. God is the embodiment of life, nature, the universe, and all that is good; whereas Satan is the personal embodiment of vastly overpowering cosmic evil.

No one escapes involvement in the clash of these divine and cosmic powers, whether it be in great world wars or in the smallest family quarrels.

The ancients even considered disease and nervous disorders, especially mental illness, traceable to the influence of evil, not entirely without reason. Somehow the Spirit of God succeeds in fashioning its masterpiece, for there is, after all, more love than hate in human affairs, more beauty than ugliness in the world, more good than evil in the whole drama of life.

The gravitational pull of man toward evil is called in theology the Doctrine of Original Sin, and the absolute need to pull against it is essential to the upward spiral of human progress.

The two greatest evils known to history are war and slavery.

The horrors of Hitlerism and the brutalities of certain crimes cannot be explained in mere human terms. They are signs of spiritual evil—the devil. The things that happened in Buchenwald, Dachau, and Auschwitz were called *The Theory and Practice of Hell* by Eugen Kogon, who came closer than perhaps even he realized to the real source of their motivation in the title for his book, based on his official reports to SHAEF. The pictures and text of his work are sickening. They are enough to make an atheist pray. Bless him!

In purely human terms we could never account for the revelations of the Manson murder trial, the behavior of Lee Harvey Oswald, Sirhan Sirhan, or the pushers who peddle heroin to our high- and even grade-school students. There is a diabolical element in all this evil—the spirit of the devil—the presence described in Miltons *Paradise Lost* as proclaiming: "Evil be thou my good."

This reversal of values is the essence of evil. It is the scriptural sense of sin. The devil has a long history of successes and defeats, too, in human affairs, from the loss of primeval innocence to the war in Vietnam.

The conflict engrosses us in the present and its impact is both frightening and personal. I believe the devil is slowly losing ground, step by step, to the creative power of God, evolving the world of the future, "our future."

My own experience with Satan, the fallen angel, Lucifer, the spirit of evil—the devil—I regard as extraordinary. It is much like that detailed in the Books of Genesis, or the Revelations of Saint John. I have related this dramatic and personal experience in *My Life and Prophecies* in the chapter on the coming of Antichrist.

"I had been in bed for hours and felt continuously on the threshold of waking and sleeping, that in-between stage when the subconscious works overtime and the conscious lies dormant, waiting for the rays of the early morning sun.

"Suddenly I sensed something moving to the right of my bed. I felt a powerful presence moving closer to me . . .

"I lay completely still, tuning my entire being into the awareness of what was happening. Then another feeling engulfed me; it was the awareness of God's love that had enveloped me to protect me from whatever was to take place.

"I looked toward the foot of my bed and saw the 'other' presence, shaped like a serpent, nudge gently against the mattress. I felt the pressure of its body increase, but it was the impact of a mental force which made me realize that it was not just a reptile. Powerful waves of intellect and majesty radiated from it; it was a mind that somehow 'took' by 'giving.'

"I remember thinking, 'What power! What intellect! . . .'" I felt as Jesus must have felt in His temptation. Such power would tempt even the God-Man!

Events have now advanced beyond the stage they had reached when those lines were written in 1964. The prophecies are on their way to fulfillment, and their mysteries will continue to unfold.

The implications of their magnitude are astounding! After living through that encounter I knew that the future symbolized in that vision was being shown to me as a climactic event in the great drama of human history, but since that time, our flights to the moon and the whole promise of future space travel have somewhat overshadowed the vision.

I thought then in that vision of "The Coming of Antichrist" and the subsequent "Child from the East" that the devil incarnate in the person of the Antichrist would be making his bid for the final mastery of man and man's world—the domination of history at its climax by a Promethean seizure of the final control of human destiny. I still believe that. But space technology from Sputnik I to Appolo XV has convinced me now that the scope of this conflict between God and the devil has widened to encompass not only human destiny, but the control of life itself.

This is the ancient enmity alluded to in Job and the Revelations. And as I know the security of God in my own life shielding me from danger even while witnessing such an apocalyptic vision, I know as well the outcome of this last great earthly contest at the frontier of eternity.

The future belongs to God.

In the words of Jesus: "I watched Satan fall from the sky like lightning." (Luke 10:18) This is not just something that happened once upon a time—or once before a time we know. It was an eternal fall ... Satan is always falling; his nature is a dynamic withdrawal into nothingness. The kingdom of hell, like the kingdom of heaven, is within, and its essence is an eternal rejection of God's love. It is self-made. There is no recovery because evil does not desire to "recover." As George Bernard Shaw observed, damnation is the state of those who love death more than life. I can only add that the choice ultimately is between eternal life and eternal death.

The Resurrection of Jesus with the prospect of His Second Coming is the divine sign that the life force in man, nature, and the world is stronger than the death force and survives it. Not only does it survive, it grows and multiplies into the universe. Should evil prevail—that is, the devil—then mortality, eternal death, would finally swallow us up in an unending night of the spirit. But since God will prevail in the Herculean struggle ahead, the way is clear for man's transfiguration in the universe according to God's design. He need only follow where the Spirit of God leads him.

Every new scientific discovery is so exciting to me it is difficult for me at times to control my enthusiasm! Imagine the earth, the cradle of life, like a tiny island in the solar system with the great undiscovered universe in the new ocean of space all around us! How glorious will our children's children be when the wars and other threats to life in this century are behind us and the next brings a brave new world undreamed of ... even by us, in our wildest dreams. It will be better than any man has ever known.

The outcome is no less than the issue between cosmic life and universal death for man; and I see a kind of super-dramatization of this in the discovery of antimatter at the frontiers of the known universe along with "anti-light" emanating from some kind of "black holes" in the sky which emit "light" waves that actually register as darkness. Somehow, by the creative action of God, matter and light, goodness and life, prevail over darkness and the void, evil, and death.

It is not, of course, entirely a cosmic, impersonal thing. Light and life, goodness and love, which inevitably involve one another, are intensely personal. The conflict with their opposites takes place not "out there" or "in human history" so much as in the deep inner life of every individual. The devil may tempt you as he tempted Jesus, and you can overcome him in the same way.

How?

By the use we make of our divinely granted talents and God-given gifts to serve humanity and heed our own call to glory. Every person is endowed by God not only with life, liberty, and certain other inalienable rights, but also with certain abilities and talents to be used in the pursuit of happiness.

If you use your intelligence to discover your divinely given talents and your energies to make them productive, you will achieve the greatest happiness possible on this earth. If you neglect these God-given talents or dissipate them merely for the sake of self-indulgence, you will be adding to the burden of evil the world must carry, which is already appalling.

I once learned the psychological lesson of the "principle of opposites," and I learned it well. It means that if you do not work to achieve a goal or strive toward an objective, you will automatically regress toward its opposite. If you do not work at being honest, friendly, constructive, you will automatically slip back toward their opposites. If you do not practice, you will never play well. If you do not develop your gifts and talents, you will become a frustrated failure, a neurotic, or even worse. As the Gospel account indicates, if you fail to worship, that is, serve God, you will be serving the devil. The final judgment will prove this beyond doubt when the "sheep" are separated from the goats, the former to enter the kingdom of the Father, the latter to be cast into eternal torment prepared for the devil and his angels (Matthew 25:31-41).

The devil? Yes! None other.

The spirit of evil is very strong in the world and steadily growing stronger. How we exercise our options for good or for evil not only decides the issues of our own lives but those of countless others.

The issue for the entire human family is now the same one faced by Israel in the time of Elijah the Prophet.

"How long will you straddle the issue?" stormed the prophet Elijah to his countrymen, when they could not make up their minds whether to serve the God of their fathers or the idol of their enemies.

"If the Lord is God, follow him," went on Elijah; "if Baal [be God], follow him." (1 Kings 18:21.)

There ensued a fearful day of weird incantation, followed by the prayer of the prophet and the intervention of God (1 Kings 18:22-40).

I believe we face the same dilemma today. We are not firm enough in our faith to follow God wholeheartedly, and not quite evil enough to follow the devil completely either.

This is what the identity crisis is all about. We are currently agonizing individually and collectively over the question of whether to identify with the transcendent will of God or the fascination of our own earthly image. The spirit of evil tempts us to love ourselves exclusively and find our fulfillment in self-centeredness; the spirit of God inspires us to transcend and humble ourselves and embrace the Infinite Being. I believe, as I have detailed in another book, that this tremendous life-and-death issue will be resolved again as it was before: by special intervention of God in earthly affairs around the end of our century ... what I interpret as divine intervention.

In this century, which has realized more suffering than any other, in which the sum total of human suffering may well have already surpassed all others combined, it is curious that so much is done for people who suffer while so little attention is given to the redemptive value of suffering itself. By the strange but ancient alchemy of human nature, it is by suffering of one sort or another that we mature and gain wisdom.

The acceptance of suffering is the beginning of wisdom!

The greatest sign of redemptive suffering is the Sign of the Cross. Those who suffer and offer their suffering to God in this spirit do more for the well-being of man than can endeavors in all the other worldly activity.

I believe this to be the reason for my final vision of God's saving intervention, which will bring peace at last to a confused, sick world. This is the Sign of the Cross, lighting the earthly sky from east to west, similar to the one seen by Constantine at the beginning of our era. The same words accompanied it: "In this sign you shall conquer ..."

The Sign of the Cross is also the sign of Jesus. It is the personal link which will join all men of goodwill after the turbulent years that lie ahead. Those who are destined to live through or take part in those tremendous events will realize as never before that we achieve our real identity by accepting our true mission from God.

Jesus expresses the lesson of the Cross clearly. It is through the Cross that true identity is discovered, we receive forgiveness and mercy from God and succeed in overcoming evil. "Whoever wishes to be my follower must deny his very self, take up his cross each day, and follow in my steps. Whoever would save his life will lose it, and whoever loses his life for my sake will save it. What profit does he show who gains the whole world and destroys himself in the process? If a man is ashamed of me and my doctrine, the Son of Man will be ashamed of him when he comes in his glory and that of his Father and his holy angels." (Luke 9:23-26.)

"It pleased God," Saint Paul assures us, "to make absolute fullness reside in him and, by means of him, to reconcile everything in his person, both on earth and in the heavens, making peace through the blood of his cross." (Colossians 1:19-20).

Our personalities become the instruments through which we express our God-appointed missions to our neighbors—or lose our identity—our "soul"—in a maze of confusion and personal chaos.

We must break through our crusted layers of egotism, prejudice, greed, and all the rest of the things that blind us to the action of God. "Get your bloated self out of the way," Emerson said, "and let divine channels through." Harsh words, perhaps, but "right on" in the spirit of today's brutally frank and honest world.

Without the willingness to face the truth of sublimating our selfish, personal interest and allowing our individual divine channels to take over in each one of us, we will never make it.

"From that time on Jesus began to proclaim this theme: 'Reform your lives! The kingdom of heaven is at hand.' As he was walking along the Sea of Galilee he watched two brothers, Simon now known as Peter, and his brother Andrew, casting a net into the sea. They were fishermen. He said to them, 'Come after me and I will make you fishers of men.' They immediately abandoned their nets and became his followers." (Matthew 4:17–20.)

If we want to get some idea of what a Church resurrected from the clutches of materialism should be like, we need only turn our attention to the little group of apostles who surrounded Jesus and helped him carry God's word to mankind.

—Jeane Dixon

9. The Apostles

Nothing in our society is as demoralizing as the wrecking of religious faith. This is because faith is the one thing necessary to fuel the human spirit; it is the good food of the soul. From it come hope and charity, which keep man ever looking for the morrow and acting like a god, at least in his best moments. If religion fails, humanity will not be far behind, for faith is the magnetic force in the iron core of human nature.

It is the point of our contact with God.

When theologians say "God is dead," they mean that divinity to the best of their knowledge and belief is no longer operative.

This is their confession of failure.

They have simply lost faith and are therefore no longer qualified to lead the human family in its vital spiritual quest. They have disqualified themselves by the words from their own mouths, and it becomes necessary for the rest of us to dismiss them from their jobs and select new leadership for the forging of our spiritual future. To begin with the song that God is dead is to sing our own requiem, for it leaves us powerless to face the problems of the cosmos and our own existence: it is the province of religion to light our way.

War is too important to leave to the generals, we say, because it involves our freedom. Economics is too important to leave to the economists because it controls our resources and their distribution. Education is too important to leave to the professors because it molds the future of our youth, and so on.

Nothing is closer to the truth than the fact that we cannot leave religion to those theologians who extol human reason instead of divine revelation as the guiding light of human life and conduct, because our very lives and existence are at stake. And it could be no more obvious from the state of the Church, the environment, the war, international relations, local politics, business, and all the rest, that they have led us into a desert.

We must have a new and devout unification of faith, lest we die! But where is such leadership to be found? Where Jesus said it would be found: in Him and in His teaching continued in and through His apostles and their successors in the Christian community for the benefit of all who accept Christ as Lord and Messiah (Matthew 28:18-20).

Some of our churches as storekeepers of the faith have failed themselves and us as well. Of course, some of us have failed the faith and the Church, too. This has in large measure contributed to the religious delinquency of our time.

Some church organizations seem to have more in common with big business than they do with Jesus' small band of apostles.

Like Peter, we can ask, when our faith and churches fail us, "Lord, to whom shall we go? You have the words of eternal life." (John 6:68.)

And the answer has not changed, because truth is one and eternal. And the Galilean fisherman's question contained its own answer: a return to Jesus in spirit and in truth, as the prototype of human nature, whom God has placed before us in history and in faith to be "the way, and the truth, and the life." (John 14:6.)

Even Jesus did not do it alone. He chose twelve apostles to help him.

If we want to get some idea of what a church resurrected from its death through egotism, materialism, technology, and bureaucracy should be like, we must turn our attention to the original reformation in Israel, to the little group of rebels who set out to bring the word of God to Israel and to the world. Far from being dead, the whole religious ideology of the past thirty-eight hundred years is still as alive and vital.

The original men who tried to revitalize the old Israel before it was torn to pieces by the Roman Empire were the Twelve: Saint Peter, appointed the chief executive officer by the Lord, and the other saints: James, John, Andrew, Philip, Thomas, Bartholomew, James the Less, Matthew, Jude, Simon, and Judas.

Of all the disciples, Simon, the one Jesus called "Peter," which means "the rock," was the most impressive. Like several of the others, Peter was a fisherman on the Sea of Galilee and lived at Capernaum on the northwestern shore. This body of water hardly merits the label "sea," for it is scarcely six miles wide and not much more than thirteen miles long. But as a place to fish and obtain food it was highly important.

Peter, like most of the other apostles, was unschooled. Nevertheless he undoubtedly had some familiarity with the ancient scriptural texts. At the time he met Jesus, Peter was probably a man in his late thirties, and it is unfortunate that artists have insisted on painting him only as an old man, usually bald, with a white beard and scraggy locks. In reality all the disciples were young, the brothers John and James being mere youths.

When Jesus began His mission, He took up residence in Peter's house, and frequently preached to the crowds on shore from Peter's boat. Thus started those momentous three years together during which a strong bond of affection grew between Jesus and His apostles, though in temperament they were worlds apart. Peter was blunt, impetuous, frank in speech, somewhat of a bungler at times, and more materialistic than mystical. For his last trait he once received a reprimand from Jesus!: "Get out of my sight, you satan! You are trying to make me trip and fall. You are not judging by God's standards but by man's.' (Matthew 16:23.)

Physically, Peter was "the big fisherman" of legend; intellectually he was otherwise. He loved Jesus as only a man without guile can love a figure of heroic spiritual stature.

How touching is the scene in Chapter Six of John's Gospel, when Jesus is prepared even for His apostles to leave Him.

"Do you want to leave me too?" Jesus said to the Twelve.

"Lord," protests Peter, "to whom shall we go? You have the words of eternal life." (John 6:67-68.)

If we carefully read the Gospels and other books of the New Testament, we can see Peter develop in spirituality and depth of understanding. To his eternal glory, it was Peter who first recognized in Jesus the promised Messiah, come to save the world.

"You are the Messiah, the Son of the living God!" he said. (Matthew 16:16.)

In return, Peter's simplicity and rugged determination represented to Jesus the kind of inspirational force needed to carry on His work. He knew this was revealed to Peter by the heavenly Father, so he said to Peter, "Blest are you, Simon son of John! No mere man has revealed this to you, but my heavenly Father. I for my part declare to you, you are 'Rock,' and on this rock I will build my church." (Matthew 16:17-18.)

The founding of the Church by Christ goes back to this beginning.

It is true that the same Peter denied his Master on the very night of the Last Supper, but at least he was there, anxious and concerned, while the other apostles, except for John, scattered to the four winds and abandoned their Master.

And how contrite Peter was shortly afterward!

"The Lord turned around and looked at Peter, and Peter remembered the word that the Lord had spoken to him, 'Before the cock crows today you will deny me three times.' He went out and wept bitterly." (Luke 22:61-62.)

How completely Peter atoned for his denial!

Following the Crucifixion, there was a miraculous transformation in that glorious, big fisherman! He became the leader, and he filled the role courageously. Suddenly he began to speak with the tongue of eloquence, and on the occasion of his very first sermon in Jerusalem he was so inspired as to bring no less than three thousand converts to Christianity.

There is nothing in Scripture to identify Peter with the Roman scene, but tradition and circumstantial evidence are so strong on this point that it is accepted that Peter eventually did go to Rome and there founded the church.

With him went a young man named John Mark, "my son Mark," at whose house in Jerusalem the Last Supper was held. Saint Mark was undoubtedly the mysterious figure present with Jesus in Gethsemane: "There was a young man following him who was covered by nothing but a linen cloth. As they seized him he left the cloth behind and ran off naked." (Mark 14:51-52.)

The presence of Mark in Rome with Peter is of supreme importance to us, for out of this experience Mark was inspired to write the second gospel, a swift-moving drama which many feel is the most accurate of the four Gospels. By then Peter was a venerable and holy patriarch, and we can imagine the young Mark listening to him and taking notes; getting it all down while there was still time.

Legend reminds us that Peter eventually despaired of making Christians out of Romans and decided to leave the city. As he made his way southward along the Appian Way, an apparition loomed up suddenly in front of him—it was the figure of his Master! The astonished Peter then uttered the famous lines: *"Quo vadis, Domine?*—Lord, where are you going?"—and Jesus said, "I am going to Rome, to finish your work for you!" On yet another occasion Jesus said: "I am going back to Rome to be crucified again."

The aging Peter, shamed as he had been so many times before, turned back toward Nero's Rome, to martyrdom and immortality.

Saint Peter's Cathedral, one of the most beautiful shrines in the world, named for him, now stands where he once preached. It is an imposing monument to a humble man, who had followed wisely and well the call heard three decades before on the mount in Galilee: "Your light must shine before men so that they may see goodness in your acts and give praise to your heavenly Father." (Matthew 5:16.)

Next in importance to Peter is Matthew (known also as Levi). Matthew was a publican, a local customs officer. There were many such government functionaries around the Sea of Galilee, for the caravan routes from the seaports to Damascus and beyond went through this region, and it was the job of the publicans to see that import levies were collected. Socially ostracized because their work was a continual reminder to the Jews of Roman domination, the publicans remained among themselves, associating only with their own kind and others upon whom society frowned. Hence, the lumping together in the Bible of "publicans and sinners."

We have no idea how it came to be that Jesus saw the potential in Matthew. But He did, and when Jesus ordered, "Follow me!" Matthew complied at once (Matthew 9:9).

But one does not quit one's profession to become a convert without celebrating the occasion, so that night Matthew celebrated by giving a dinner, at which Jesus sat down to eat and drink with the publicans and sinners. "What reason can the Teacher have for eating with tax collectors and those who disregard the law?" asked the Pharisees. "Overhearing the remark, he [Jesus] said: 'People who are in good health do not need a doctor; sick people do.'" (Matthew 9:11-12.)

Christians revere Saint Matthew as the author of the first gospel, certainly one of the most remarkable books in the history of mankind. In this inspired text, so beautifully phrased and so profoundly spiritual, Matthew, more personally than the other three, Mark, Luke and John, caught the essence of the divine message, the true nature of Jesus' personality, and the nobility of His character. It was Matthew who gave us the great discourses (he alone groups together several discourses of Jesus into the one Sermon on the Mount): He also portrays Jesus as a man of His time, living out the drama of His life among contemporary forces, inveighing against evils as He saw them, and Jesus finally the victim of forces and circumstances peculiar to His time and society.

We lose sight of Matthew after the Crucifixion, but tradition says he went about preaching for fifteen years in Palestine and after this to foreign nations; the Ethiopians, Macedonians, Syrians, Parthians, and Medes are mentioned. Another story has him campaigning for Christ in northern Persia, where he was finally put to death, one more dedicated "sheep in the midst of wolves."

Andrew, Peter's brother, is the patron saint of Scot-

land and, like him, was a fisherman. Andrew made little
stir among the tightly knit group of apostles; no doubt
the forthrightness of his commanding brother overshadowed him. Following the Crucifixion, we must depend on
legend to follow this apostle, for he is mentioned only
once in the Book of Acts, Chapter One, and never again
in the various epistles.

Andrew seems to have first been a follower of John the
Baptist and later became one of the Twelve who followed Jesus. We can imagine the lively discussions between the Lord and Andrew, with Andrew recalling a
more rigid doctrine under John, and, despite his loyalty,
even questioning the more relaxed attitudes of his new
Teacher.

Like the others, Andrew continued His Master's work
following the Crucifixion. Andrew is said to have
preached in Greece and Scythia, and was reportedly
martyred in Patrae in 70 A.D.

James and John were the sons of a prosperous fisherman named Zebedee. Evidently they were young
hotheads, for Jesus nicknamed them "sons of thunder,"
and apparently had His troubles with these two. Once,
while crossing the unfriendly territory of Samaria, Jesus
and the apostles were made unwelcome in a certain
town, and the "sons of thunder" suggested: "Lord, would
you not have us call down fire from heaven to destroy
them?" (Luke 9:54.) Jesus, the Prince of Peace, repri-
manded them, telling them in effect to "cool it."

Would that He were here today in person to repeat
that message to those who want to "burn down the
town!"

For He would say to them: "Cool it" ... and they
would indeed cool it!

For such is the loving persuasion of Jesus, and the
enormous importance of His message, that none—then or
now—can afford to ignore it.

John and James, along with Peter, formed an inner

circle, a sort of cabinet. Only these three accompanied Jesus on the day of the Transfiguration; only they remained close to Him while He prayed in Gethsemane.

Saint John, in his gospel, assigns to himself a special place in the esteem of Jesus; he refers to himself as "the disciple whom Jesus loved" (John 13:23). It seems that John, being the youngest of the apostles, with a naive and affectionate nature, did inspire paternal feelings in our Lord. In John's version of the scene on Calvary, Jesus, from the Cross, entrusts His mother to John's care. John should be a son to Mary, she a mother to him. Jesus' wishes were carried out.

When all the other apostles were gone, John was still around, no longer a firebrand, but an old and serenely dignified holy man, living in a cave on the isle of Patmos, to which he had been exiled. There he wrote the Book of Revelation, a wondrous, prophetic treatise so full of the mystical that generation after generation has tried unsuccessfully to clarify all its mysteries. With time, however, parts of it are made clear, and with more time, all of the mysteries will be made clear.

James, brother of John, had a different destiny. After the Crucifixion, James remained in Jerusalem, working with Peter and the others to get the new Church established. Frequently referred to as Saint James the Greater, this apostle finally ran afoul of Herod Agrippa (grandson of the cruel Herod the Great), who had him executed (Acts 12:2).

A touching legend which surrounds the death of Saint James tells how the remains of the saint were miraculously conveyed to Spain, landing near Compostela.

Saint James has been the patron saint of Spain ever since.

Philip was also a fisherman, born at Bethsaida, on the north side of the lake. He responded at once to Jesus' invitation to follow Him and then proceeded to seek out Nathanael to tell him: "We have found the one Moses spoke of in the law—the prophets too—Jesus, son of Joseph, from Nazareth," wishing thereby to share his faith and trust. When Nathanael questioned the possibility of anything good coming from Nazareth, Philip urgently invited him to see for himself (John 1:43-46).

On the occasion of the multiplication of the loaves and fishes, Jesus, seeing the crowd coming toward Him, said to Philip: "Where shall we buy bread for these people to eat?" Philip replied: "Not even with two hundred days' wages could we buy loaves enough to give each of them a mouthful!" (John 6:5-7.)

Again, the Greeks who came to Jerusalem to worship on the Passover feast approached Philip that through him they might get to see Jesus. He in turn asked Andrew to accompany him as he introduced them to Jesus (John 12:20-22).

During the beautiful last discourse of Jesus to His disciples, in which He spoke so fervently of His Father, it was Philip again who said: "Lord, show us the Father and that will be enough for us." To which Jesus replied: "Philip, after I have been with you all this time, you still do not know me? Whoever has seen me has seen the Father. . . . Believe me that I am in the Father and the Father is in me." (John 14:8-9, 11.)

Thus Philip shows himself a colorful figure thoroughly taken up with Jesus and His work during the days he spent with the Master. To find God in finding Jesus is the great lesson he occasioned for all of us (John 14:9).

Thomas or Didymus was an appealing sort of fellow. We know little about this man, save the fact that he was very skeptical and gave birth to the phrase "doubting Thomas." We do not know his profession, nor his place of origin, and he is mentioned only a few times in Scripture. We do know that Thomas insisted upon touching the flesh and even the wounds of our Lord following the Resurrection before he would believe Christ truly had risen from the grave. Once convinced, he was as dedicated as the others. When the Lord appeared before him and to still his unbelief said, "Take your finger and examine my hands. Put your hand into my side. Do not persist in your unbelief, but believe!" Thomas fell to his knees and in the humblest of supplications, answered, "My Lord and my God." (John 20:27-28).

And from then on Saint Thomas had no more doubts about Him.

He had gotten to know Jesus!

We lose sight of Saint Thomas following the meeting of the apostles described in Chapter One of Acts, but the legends surrounding his later life are extraordinarily thrilling. He is said to have spent his last days as a missionary in India, and to this day there exists a Christian sect in that country which claims Saint Thomas as its founder. According to another legend, Saint Thomas was martyred at a place called Mylapore, the date unknown. One begins to see how prophetic were the words of Jesus to His apostles: "You will be hated by all on account of me." (Matthew 10:22.)

Bartholomew, meaning "son of Tolmar" (or Nathanael), was of the town of Cana, a few miles from Nazareth, where Jesus performed the gracious miracle of changing water into wine. Assuming that Bartholomew is the Nathanael spoken of in Chapter One of the Gospel according to Saint John, this apostle appears to have started off on the wrong foot with Jesus. When Philip told Bartholomew that he had found the new Messiah, who came from Nazareth, Bartholomew made his famous remark, "Can anything good come from Nazareth?" (John 1:46.) Nazareth, the small hometown of Jesus, was frequently the target of jokes.

According to tradition, Saint Bartholomew preached extensively throughout Arabia, where he was eventually put to death as an agitator. The knife, with which he was flayed to death, remains today the symbol of the martyred Saint Bartholomew.

James the Less was the son of Alphaeus, and whether it was simply a coincidence or not, Alphaeus was also the name of Matthew's father. Were they brothers? History does not record.

Saint James the Less, according to the scant information available, became the first Christian bishop of Jerusalem and is said to have been thrown from the roof of the temple to his death there by anti-Christians in 62 A.D. He is the author of the epistle bearing his name. It is notable for its denouncement in strong terms of prejudice and snobbery.

Saint Jude was also identified in the Bible as Thaddeus, or Lebbaeus. He wrote the short epistle found near the end of the New Testament. It is believed he preached in Persia, where he suffered martyrdom along with Saint Simon. Jude is represented in art by a staff and carpenter's square, indicating that he followed the same trade as Jesus.

Simon the Zealot has always been a controversial figure among the apostles because of the nickname he bore. He was not a fisherman, but a fishmonger (one who buys and sells fish).

Saint Simon continued after Christ's Resurrection "to go and preach," being martyred with Saint Jude in Persia.

And now, to the last of the apostles, Judas Iscariot. Judas has been called the one contradictory figure in the story of our Lord, and with reason. First, he was not from Galilee; all the other apostles were. Instead, he came from a small town in the very south of Judea called Kerioth. Who was he, and how did he come to join the Twelve? The answer may be of such utter simplicity that down through the years men have failed to see it.

Jesus and His group needed Judas Iscariot. Though the individual apostles were capable of handling their own uncomplicated affairs, when it came to looking out for thirteen persons all at once, they needed an accountant—someone to keep an account of things, buy provisions, and manage the purse strings. There was a practical side to the ministry of our Lord, just as there exists today a practical or business aspect of the ministry. A skilled accountant they found in Judas Iscariot. As a Judean, Judas did not appeal to the Galileans, and vice-versa. The two districts had been at loggerheads for centuries. In addition, it seems Judas laid claim to noble blood, another source of irritation to the rustic Galileans.

These, then, were the men Jesus gathered around Him. Coming from various walks of life, the one thing they had in common was wonderful affection and boundless admiration for their Leader. In reality, the formation and establishment of this loyal group was the great work of Jesus, for without their dedicated campaigns, Christianity would have died aborning.

Complete acceptance and love for the living resurrected Jesus and all He taught was the basic creed the Twelve followed; the memory of Jesus and His noble precepts they carried to their graves. These men, through Jesus, brought a new spirit into the world, a love disassociated from all evil, distinguished by its unblemished purity and simple principles.

In substance, Jesus and His small group constituted in their own little world, the whole world as God envisioned it should be in principle—loving God and one another, keeping His laws, sharing talents, and avoiding self-centeredness, which is the basic source of sin.

It was the vision of a new era, in which the Church would take this vision of Israel to all the world, "to all nations," and "to every creature."

For a while this preaching was done very well by the apostles and their successors. In accordance with the design of Jesus, the Church He founded grew to include people of every age and race, justifying what Paul said of the believers, that "There does not exist among you Jew or Greek, slave or freeman, male or female. All are one in Christ Jesus." (Galatians 3:28.) It freed peoples whenever it could. The vision was an overwhelming one, and it worked so well it gathered a momentum that proved irresistible. It could not be stopped.

Jesus guaranteed freedom from defect to His Church which, inasmuch as it is a divine institution built by Christ on Peter the Rock, would never be overcome by the power or forces of evil (Matthew 16:18-19). Nevertheless, this was no guarantee of sinlessness to individual members, as the long history of the Church abundantly shows.

In our time, wishing to restore the freshness and fervor of spirit of the early Church and to adapt it to the circumstances of life today, Pope John, his successor Pope Paul, the World Council of Churches, the governing boards of rabbis, and various independents like the Reverend Billy Graham have made attempts to dam the flood of confusion, avarice, and despair that have followed the wars and persecutions of our century. They have generated or preserved an intense if vestigial religious faith, a yearning for the return of charity and brotherhood, and above all, a desperate Messianic hope!

It is of that hope I speak now amidst the poisons polluting the spring of our faith.

In an Elijan age of prophecy false teachers would have been led down to the brook Kishon to have their throats cut, but perhaps we live in more merciful times (1 Kings 18:40). If we forgive even Judas, how can we refuse the same courtesy to such false teachers of today? Perhaps forgiving their faults and praying for them will reconstitute their respect for the lessons of Scripture, their reverence for the name of God and the faith to which they were called! If we will do penance for our sins, Like Jonas for Nineveh, perhaps our cities will yet be saved!

I foresee the end of the religious crisis of our century. I have written about it in full elsewhere. The ecumenical movement is full of good intentions to pull itself together; but things have gone too far for it to succeed without the divine intervention of God.

I believe there will be such a divine intervention before the year 2050, but not before the martyrdom of another Pope and the deaths of millions in war. It is all so horrible and so unnecessary!

How wonderful if we would turn to God and, through faith and prayer, end the religious crisis without the necessity of divine intervention!

As Eric Sevareid observed one night with what seemed to me divine insight: "People, when they learn at all, learn the hard way, and then generally too late."

I believe they will again learn the hard way, but hopefully, not entirely too late.

"Whoever does the will of my heavenly Father is brother and sister and mother to me." (Matthew 12:50.)

If only women understood the message of Jesus of which they are so vital a part, they could save the world!
—Jeane Dixon

10. Jesus and Women

Women deeply revered Jesus of Nazareth. He was a superior Being radiating a divine charisma, a fascinating magnetism incredibly free of prejudice. He treated women as equals, asking nothing of them for Himself but seeking their love for God the Father. Jesus was a normal man, but also one who was free of sin and consequently of the desires resulting from sin. Unlike the ordinary man who finds such sublimation incomprehensible, Jesus could say, "Some men are incapable of sexual activity from birth; some have been deliberately made so; and some there are who have freely renounced sex for the sake of God's reign." (Matthew 19:12.)

The very fact of His chastity made Jesus appealing to all types of women. In His presence they could relax and feel free with Him. It was not necessary to play the mating game, to watch everything one said or did. Like a true brother He loved them and listened to their problems, advised them well and asked no favors in return. No doubt to some He became the unattainable ideal, immune to sensuality, but withal kind, gentle, and sensitive. Though men and women will always be eternal mysteries to each other, Jesus was even more so, for in Him unquestioned masculinity went hand in hand with steadfast celibacy.

Giovanni Papini wrote: "Jesus had over women the

inestimable prestige of innocence." Perhaps that was the secret of His charm—innocence.

Two personalities live side by side in women, the mother and the wife. A mother's concern is with innocence, a maternal love totally unselfish. Did the adoring women who surrounded Jesus think of Him maternally, as one too preoccupied with spirituality to think of women as an opposite sex? And did not Jesus perhaps think of women, too, as children, adrift in a world not really kind to them, not concerned with understanding them as human beings?

No one realized better than Jesus how demeaning was the role of women in His day. His life was a mandate of respect for the rights and privileges of all—women included. A new attitude toward women was one of the most powerful attractions of the early Christian Church. Women converts enjoyed the beginnings of the emancipation of their sex, and indeed, even if Christ's only contribution to history had been a new concept of sexual dignity, His life would have been memorable!

Moses had attempted to achieve fairness for women in the law of the land, but had not succeeded, and in practice throughout biblical times the woman's role was inferior. Even Mosaic law could be harsh; read Leviticus, Chapter Twelve, and you find that a woman who gave birth to a boy was considered "unclean" for seven days and in isolation for thirty-three days, while the birth of a girl made her "unclean" for fourteen days and isolated for sixty-six days!

Nevertheless, the only real merit for women in those days was in motherhood. Sterility was not only shameful, the prospect of being barren was absolutely frightening to Hebrew women. Listen to the cry of despairing Rachel: "Give me children, or I shall die!" (Genesis 30:1.) Recall the anguish of Abraham's wife Sarah when she realized she was barren. Her only recourse was to have a "proxy" child by her Egyptian maid Hagar

(Genesis 16), a degrading practice later followed by Jacob, who fathered children by the two maids of both his wives when it appeared they both were sterile (Genesis 30:1-24). This practice of fathering children by other women when the wife was barren was evidently common in Israel as in most of the ancient world.

One should add that all three wives mentioned above eventually had children.

Most of the biblical stories involving women show them in unfavorable roles, none of which was lost on Jesus. For instance, the story of Ruth, touching as it is, in reality depicts a supplicating female seeking the favor of a dominant male. Judith, a great heroine, had "to play the harlot" in order to get close enough to the dreaded Assyrian general Holofernes to slay him. Likewise the story of Esther—her success with King Ahasuerus came about when she used the only weapons available to her, her beauty and sex.

One could go on and on citing the abasement of women in biblical days.

One of the most flagrant instances was the violation of Tamar by her half-brother Ammon, both children of King David. Following the despicable assault, Ammon went his way unconcerned, but, as the Second Book of Samuel tells us, in shame and humiliation the *innocent* Tamar "put ashes on her head and tore the long tunic in which she was clothed. Then, putting her hands to her head, she went away crying loudly." (2 Samuel 13:19.) Obviously, it was a man's world! However, Ammon later paid the penalty in full—with his life (2 Samuel 13:32).

The intolerable status of women had a psychological effect (not altogether unexpected). As they have always done in male-dominated societies, women began to employ feminine wiles to obtain what they desired, and as a result many men in Israel became suspicious of womankind in general. Page after page in Scripture warns against "the perfidious sex."

The author of Ecclesiastes declares: "More bitter than death I find the woman who is a hunter's trap, whose heart is a snare and whose hands are prison bonds.... One man out of a thousand have I come upon, but a woman among them all I have not found." (Ecclesiastes 7:26-28.)

As long as men and women honor each other according to the requirements of nature there will be no conflict. The enslavement of women and the inferior place forced upon her even in "enlightened" societies are aberrations of the natural order. Jesus of Nazareth knew this, and the actions of His life show the clarity of His intellect and the purity of His understanding. With Him there is no necessity of emphasizing "equality" or "liberation," because there is no inequality or enslavement. Women's liberation, youth protest, black militance, and such movements are only outraged demands that "Christian" societies make good on their promise. Men and woman have roles in nature that are equal and complementary. Jesus simply acted on this assumption, even going so far as to insist upon the right to remain single if one chose, without discrimination.

In Deuteronomy, Chapter Twenty-two, we learn how a maiden could be put through the degrading ordeal of proving virginity when a new husband doubted. The episode between Judah and his daughter-in-law Tamar, told in Chapter Thirty-eight of Genesis, indicated strongly that a woman was believed guilty until proven otherwise, a premise one finds echoed in the story of Susannah and the "Peeping Elders" (Daniel 13).

In addition to His divine intuition that God repudiated such debasement, some of Christ's most compelling and inspirational lessons involve women. Undoubtedly the most famous is the episode of The Woman Taken in Adultery (John 8:1-11). The incident is considered to be the primary lesson on forgiveness: that we should not condemn others since we ourselves have so much for which we should be forgiven.

However, Jesus saw much deeper meaning. A woman had been caught in an adulterous act, and the elders were ready to stone her to death. The law, as propounded by Moses, was clear: "If a man commits adultery with his neighbor's wife, both the adulterer and the adulteress shall be put to death." (Leviticus 20:10.) Where was the man in the case? In practice it did not always work out that both adulterers were punished, and Jesus knew it.

During that final and fatal week in Jerusalem an incident took place which Jesus used to illustrate one of his strongest lessons. It was a minor incident, scarcely meriting attention, but Jesus saw in it a powerful means to show how hypocritical were the rich and the powerful with their lip service to God. On the one hand wealthy bankers, lawyers, government officials; on the other a poor widow—each donating to the temple treasury. Jesus watched the rich drop in their offerings, and then he saw the widow, humble in her approach, drop in two small coins, emptying her purse.

"I want you to observe," He said to the disciples, "that this poor widow contributed more than all the others who donated to the treasury. They gave from their surplus wealth, but she gave from her want, all that she had to live on." Jesus saw in this sacrifice her *complete* devotion to God, not just a patronizing gesture like the donations of the mighty.

Jesus envisioned women *as powerful allies* in propagating the word of God. He knew, as did some of the later saints, that one convinced woman was worth a platoon of halfhearted males, that one could count on their faith being steadfast, their assistance valuable and selfless. Along with their allegiance, women provided Jesus and His disciples with the money and food needed to travel around Israel preaching to the multitudes. The Gospel is not reticent about this. We read in Luke, Chapter Eight, this quaint reference: "... and also some women who had been cured of evil spirits and maladies: Mary called the Magdalene, from whom seven devils had gone out, Joanna, the wife of Herod's steward Chuza, Susanna, *and many others* who were assisting them out of their means." (Luke 8:2-3.)

Once people had begun to assist Him and to accept His message, Jesus sought a wider following. As a start toward universality, He saw the possibility of reaching the hostile Samaritans. We who believe in the divinity of Christ know that God the Father guided the actions of Jesus. But even those who consider Jesus just an ordinary man, though certainly an inspired one, admit that the incident with The Woman at the Well (the Samaritan woman) was the vanguard to the world beyond. She occasioned Jesus' advance into the broader development of His role, eliciting His initial move toward universality. As His words to His apostles showed, she opened a new field of His mission.

She was a local woman, this woman of Samaria, and certainly not outstanding in any way. Her nature was evidently both curious and sensual. She had had five husbands and was living with a sixth man to whom she was not married. And here we have the ineffable beauty of Christ's teaching: the woman was a sinner by the standards of her society as well as His, but Jesus saw worth in her, as He did in everyone.

But Jesus taught that through sincere repentance comes forgiveness, and He was ever ready to forgive.

Read the conversation in John, Chapter Four, between the Samaritan woman and Jesus.

"Give me a drink," said Jesus.

"You are a Jew. How can you ask me, a Samaritan and a woman, for a drink?"

"If only you recognized God's gift, and who it is that

is asking you for a drink, you would have asked him instead, and he would have given you living water. . . . Everyone who drinks this water will be thirsty again. But whoever drinks the water I give him will never be thirsty." (John 4:7-10, 13-14.)

They speak further, she stressing the Samaritan manner of worshiping Yahweh, the tribal God of the Hebrews, and he mystifying her by exposing fully her marital situation. "You people worship what you do not understand . . . an hour is coming, and is already here, when authentic worshipers will worship the Father in Spirit and truth." (John 4:22-23.)

The woman is puzzled, naturally, for the stranger proceeds to tell her all about her mixed-up domestic life. She rushes home to retell the story: "Come and see someone who told me everything I ever did. Could this not be the Messiah?" (John 4:29.)

Jesus preached to the crowd of Samaritans who gathered to see the man who brought the water of life. "No longer does our faith depend on your story. We have heard for ourselves, and we know that this really is the Savior of the world." (John 4:42.)

A woman, and an unconventional one at that, *opens up for the very first time the outside world*—the world beyond Judea and Galilee. The word of God is making progress! And it will make further progress—*through another woman!*

It was a tense time for Jesus. The agents of Herod Antipas were out to apprehend Him, and His life was in imminent danger. Accompanied by His apostles, Jesus fled to safety northward, into present-day Lebanon. His reputation as preacher and healer had preceded Him, and everywhere crowds gathered when He appeared.

The afflicted sought His aid. Among these was a Phoenician woman, whose daughter was deathly ill. She begged Jesus to cast the devil out of her child. Jesus said to the woman, "My mission is only to the lost sheep of the house of Israel. . . . It is not right to take the food of sons and daughters and throw it to the dogs."

The woman, not to be put off, said: "Please, Lord, even the dogs eat the leavings that fall from their masters' tables." (Matthew 15:24-27.)

I believe this was one of the transcendental moments in the life of our Lord. Jesus was tired, discouraged by the turn of events, an exile from His own land. He reacted rather crossly, but the woman of Canaan by the directness of her appeal and the depth of her faith persisted and finally communicated her desperation to Jesus.

First, there was the woman of Samaria, not a Jew, who by her quick acceptance of Jesus, had turned His thoughts to a broader fulfillment of His mission; and now the woman of Canaan demonstrates that other than Jews can share in the kingdom of God. Is this perhaps the moment when our Lord decides once and for all that the glory of God is far too resplendent to remain confined within the borders of Jewry? He accepts the challenge beyond His ethnic frontier. "Woman," He says to her, "you have great faith! Your wish will come to pass." That very moment her daughter got better.

During His final week, the week of the Crucifixion, when Jesus was denied and betrayed, it was *only the women,* save one man who remained faithful! The only faithful apostle beneath the Cross was Saint John. On the very day of Crucifixion as the tragic procession made its way along the Street of Sorrows, "A great crowd of people followed him, including women who beat their breasts and lamented over him." (Luke 23:27.) As Jesus strained under the awful weight of the Cross, according to legend a woman named Veronica stepped from the crowd and wiped His face with her veil. Despite His agony, Jesus was pained to see the women weeping. Stopping momentarily, unmindful of the soldier's prod, He addresses them: "Daughters of Jerusalem, do not weep for me. Weep for yourselves and for your children." (Luke 23:28.)

At the place of execution, "Many women were present looking on from a distance. They had followed Jesus from Galilee to attend to his needs. Among them were Mary Magdalene, and Mary the mother of James and Joseph, and the mother of Zebedee's sons." (Matthew 27:55-56.)

Faithful to the very end, each would willingly have suffered with Him. As Jesus had shown appreciation for them, they responded in kind. Because He endowed their sex with the dignity and esteem God intended they should have, the women surrounded Him with warmth and affection, and even devotion.

There can be no doubt that, in turn, He found inspiration in them. "The Teacher is here, asking for you," said Martha to her sister Mary (John 11:28). Still it was Martha herself whom Jesus addressed and responded to at the tomb of Lazarus. Although He treated each woman He met in the record of Scripture as a unique creation of God, Martha and Mary of Bethany were His favorites. They thought of Him as confidant and friend. He favored them with His informal company, and they favored Him with theirs. Being a normal man, He enjoyed their companionship with or without Lazarus, from their little domestic complaints to their grief and mourning when death stilled a loved one. They were very much at home together, and there is every indication that their friendship ranks among the great ones in history.

From then on the women behind every great man had their counterparts in the women close to Jesus of Nazareth. No harm ever came to Him from any one of them.

In the mind of Jesus the idea of woman was the prototype of that in the mind of the Creator described in early Genesis. She was beautiful, intelligent, honest, and loving. She was and is the complement of man.

What did He mean: "Weep for yourselves and for your children"? Why weep for them?

Because He knew what was coming: the destruction of the city and its inhabitants. Foreseeing in vision the rejection of His divine mission by His people and the terrible consequences it would have for them, in the very moment of His triumphal entry into Jerusalem on Palm Sunday, Saint Luke tells us: "Coming within sight of the city, he wept over it and said: 'If only you had known the path to peace this day; but you have completely lost it from view! Days will come upon you when your enemies encircle you with a rampart, hem you in, and press you hard from every side. They will wipe you out, you and your children within your walls, and leave not a stone on a stone within you, because you failed to recognize the time of your visitation.' " (Luke 19:41-44.)

That was why Jesus had said, "Weep for yourselves and for your children." For it was in the lifetime of many of these women and children that the prophecy was fulfilled. In 70 A.D. the Roman legions came to Jerusalem and utterly destroyed it. The ruins of the temple remain to this day. Hardly anyone survived in the besieged city, and the horrible accounts of its last days tell of how even cannibalism broke out among the few survivors before the Romans finally entered the sacred precincts and leveled everything within. This was a divine intervention in human history, foreseen and foretold by Jesus, and it came because His people had "not known the time of their visitation."

Do we know the time of our visitation, now, in these days when some men live like kings in a paradise of pleasures which for many is almost beyond imagination?

How are we using these gifts of God, given to us for the glory of His name and the service of our neighbor?

Jesus spoke of this intervention of God many times. Saint Matthew relates another occasion in which He admonishes His people: "Jerusalem, Jerusalem," He cried, "murderess of prophets and stoner of those who were sent to you! How often have I yearned to gather your children, as a mother bird gathers her young under her wings, but you refused me. . . . 'You will find your temple deserted.' " (Matthew 23:37-38.)

How do we know that this is actually what Jesus meant?

The gospel of Saint Luke tells it all. In Chapter Twenty-three we read: "Jesus turned to them and said, 'Daughters of Jerusalem, do not weep for me. Weep for yourselves and for your children. The days are coming when they will say, 'Happy are the sterile, the wombs that never bore and the breasts that never nursed.' Then will they begin saying to the mountains, 'Fall on us,' and to the hills, 'Cover us.' If they do these things in the green wood, what will happen in the dry?" (Luke 23:28-31.)

Jesus saw the destruction of Jerusalem clearly in prophetic vision with the insight of divinity. His words were an accurate description of what actually followed in less than half a century, because His people were unaware of their "visitation." Since they ignored the visitation of the Messiah, Jesus saw the inevitable divine intervention that would follow.

This was a revelation.

The meaning of this saying of Jesus' is that if innocence meets such a fate, what will happen to the guilty.

The "green wood" is Jesus, and all who follow His teaching in faith and truth and love of God. These too are the faithful Jerusalem whose sufferings help to save the world. The "dry wood" are all those who lack these virtues, like many in the ancient Jerusalem, and are thereby liable to the punishments symbolized by the cry that the mountains should fall on them and the hills cover them. The same parallel applies today, and I am able to confirm it with a similar revelation. Our world today faces the same decision with the same consequences. We can accept Jesus with His divine message from God, or we can turn our backs on God and go our own way.

Our world of confusion, evil, and conflict is the "dry wood" to which Jesus still speaks, as He spoke to His own people in His own time. The essence of His message was to live for the good and service of others rather than for selfish ends. That was why He thought of the women and their children before Himself, even though He was on His way to suffering and death! His thoughts were still first with the women, His people who were crucifying Him and those who would come after them. If only we could understand that! "It is not to do my own will that I have come down from heaven," he had said, "but to do the will of him who sent me." (John 6:38.) How truly He was acting out His own words!

This time, in the reintervention of God in human history which I see coming, His message *will be accepted*. But the intervention of God to come will be much more forceful than was the ancient destruction of Jerusalem. Instead of God's destruction of the old Jerusalem as a sign of vengeance for the rejected Messiah, it will be destruction in the world and eventual rebirth of the new world prophesied. This destructive prelude to God's reign in the world will come about because of the world's rejection of Jesus, much as His own people rejected Him at His first coming.

If only the women of that day had understood the words of the Man for whom they wept! If only they had recognized the Messiah, they could have saved their city and the great tragedy of Calvary. But, while they felt compassion for the figure of the suffering Prophet going to His death, they did not fully comprehend the tremendous drama of which they were so vital a part. If only the women of our day could understand the message of Jesus of which they are so vital a part, *they could save the world!* But though they may weep tears of compassion for Jesus like the women of old, they are still only tears of compassion and not "tears of vision."

As a result of this lack of vision we have been wasting our God-given talents—our divinely granted talents—squandering and destroying our lives and our resources, carelessly, pursuing follies of our own invention. We think we are so sophisticated and clever! Actually, we are using our talents to destroy ourselves through jealousy, greed, and envy. If only we could see with the vision of Jesus how foolish we are! Running after illusions and novelties instead of developing our gifts to the full in the service of all, we have created divisions among nations, races, and peoples which lead us from one conflict to another.

The wars which have grown in violence and deadliness since the Romans sacked Jerusalem have reached such magnitude and devastating force today that only an intervention of God in history will save us again from destroying ourselves altogether. Peace will not be won on the field of battle: Yes, peace will be ours, but by divine intervention. This will be the final version of the promise of Jesus: " 'Peace' is my farewell to you, my peace is my gift to you; I do not give it to you as the world gives peace." (John 14:27.) This is the peace that comes with understanding and love.

"Stand fast, with the truth as the belt around your waist, justice as your breastplate, and zeal to propagate the gospel of peace as your footgear. In all circumstances hold faith up before you as your shield; it will help you extinguish the fiery darts of the evil one." (Ephesians 6:14–16.)

It is in the quiet solitude of an honest and contrite heart that you will find the key to living by faith.

—Jeane Dixon

11. Living by Faith

If I stood on the west bank of the Suez Canal and stretched my arm out over the water toward the Sinai Peninsula, I know nothing would happen. Even if I had the original rod of Moses, I know I could stand there forever and the canal would dry up before anything unusual would occur.

But if I were Moses himself and the Suez Canal were the ancient "Sea of Reeds" (the Red Sea) and there were a few million Jews behind me praying for survival with a rampant Egyptian army behind them preparing to butcher them all, I also know what would happen: the wind would blow worse than any hurricane, the waters would swirl back upon themselves and over the land as the Long Island Sound did over Fire Island in 1954, and the Jews would flee pell mell through the reeds while the Egyptians would be surprised to find themselves inundated by the flood and swept to a watery grave.

I doubt very much that Moses was surprised by what happened any more than I am surprised when something foreseen in prayer actually happens; you learn to expect it.

If Moses stretched forth his rod over the reeds and waters and nothing had happened, Moses would have known that either he or the Jews had failed, not God. I know exactly how he felt at Meribah when he struck the

121

rock with his rod to produce water, and nothing happened. Utter astonishment! Who had failed, Moses or his people? Both, in different ways, and he knew it. But he did not give up: he struck the rock again, water gushed forth, and the people of God were saved again! This is an example of "living by faith." But you never can be sure, being human, that you will not fail; if you do fail, you can be sure you will get another chance if you persevere, like Moses at the Waters of Contradiction.

Like any other accomplishment, living by faith takes constant practice.

You have to practice every day to become good at it. After years of practicing you are not surprised at the power of faith, but only how anyone gets along without it! That is the stage when faith begins to pass from the realm of belief to the greater assurance of knowledge or experience. Yet you never reach it fully, as an artist or musician approaches perfection but never quite reaches it. I knew when I met my husband for the first time that I would marry him; yet when there was a rumor that he had been killed in an automobile accident I had to call him and hear his voice to be sure that I was right and the reports were wrong! When I "see" something happening in the future, unless of course it is a revelation, I must allow for misinterpretation on my part and for people changing their minds.

This comes long after faith has passed on to the realm of knowledge and experience, although the transition is never complete. I "believe" in God not because I read about faith somewhere or because I was convinced by the logic of Saint Thomas Aquinas's "proofs" of the existence of God. I "believe" in God because I feel I have known God personally in various ways since I was five years of age. Since then I have met God every day of my life in some way, sometimes in the house, on the street, sometimes in an airplane, on the highway, in a train or in other people. Mostly I meet God in prayer, in thought, in the depths of my own soul, or in the solitude of a quiet church. So do millions of others. Although the gift of prophecy is rare, the gift of prayer is not. Through the gift of faith anyone can cultivate a life of prayer—they go together—just as anyone can learn to read and write. With it comes development of your spiritual talent.

It is not possible to know God as you know your best friend, because God and humans are not equals. We can be good friends on a personal basis with God as long as we remember He is our "Almighty God." God respects your wishes, and to keep the friendship you must return the courtesy. Otherwise you will hear from Him less often.

Pascal wrote, "It is the heart which experiences God, and not the reason." How true this is! For the infinite God, like time without end, or space without limit, is much too big a concept for human minds to grasp. Therefore one finds divine intelligence active in such things as the beauty of flowers, the birth of a child, or the marvelously ordered plan of the heavens. These wondrous things are more comprehensible when we have faith in God.

The mere fact that we were born and live should give us faith in God, but often it does not; so what solidifies the true Christian's belief? It is the reality of Jesus, the divine Son of His heavenly Father whom God in His wisdom sent into the world not only for the remission of our sins, but to open our eyes to true belief.

We need faith today, for upon the basic belief in God are structured all our other beliefs. On May 24, 1844, Samuel F. B. Morse changed history when he sent the very first telegraph message between Washington and Baltimore: "What hath God wrought!" Our astronauts exemplified this again so beautifully when they reached the moon: God was praised.

We achieve all sorts of wonders today in science, technology, and medicine, but man only unlocks and discovers these marvels; he does not create them. Only God can do that!

Faith in God implies discipline; there are standards to go by in faith just as there are in science. Believers are disciplined people, respectful of the rights and property of others and, in some ways most important, respectful of themselves. The breakdown of our society today, the erosion of the quality of our lives, is unquestionably tied in with the decline of religious faith. Without faith, there is no fear of justice, no accounting for transgressions, and this irresponsible attitude is the historic road to anarchy. Without faith there is no integrity, and the great example of Jesus that we should love one another becomes distorted.

How much drama we see in the story of Jesus, and how many stirring episodes are tied in with faith! "The man who hears my word and has faith in him who sent me possesses eternal life," said Jesus. And Saint Paul echoed this in his Epistle to the Hebrews: "Let us hold unswervingly to our profession which gives us hope, for he who made the promise deserves our trust." (Hebrews 10:23.)

Do you recall the incident of the epileptic boy? The lad's father had appealed first to the disciples, but they were unable to effect a cure. In desperation the distraught man appealed directly to Jesus.

"If out of the kindness of your heart you can do anything to help us, please do!" he pleaded, to which Jesus replied, "Everything is possible to a man who trusts." (Mark 9:22-23.) The boy's father immediately exclaimed, "I do believe! Help my lack of trust!" (Mark 9:24.) Our Lord, recognizing the man's sincerity, cured the child.

When the disciples asked why they had not been able to do the same, Jesus said, "Because you have so little trust.... I assure you, if you had faith the size of a mustard seed, you would be able to say to this mountain, 'Move from here to there,' and it would move. Nothing would be impossible for you." (Matthew 17:20.)

Then there is the story of the ten lepers, as told in Luke, Chapter Seventeen. Leprosy was a terrible curse in those days, for those afflicted with the loathsome disease were driven off to live out their lives in isolation, forced to signal their approach by shouting "unclean, unclean," and doomed to exist on scraps of food thrown to them by relatives or neighbors.

One day, as Jesus made His way along the route skirting Samaria, He encountered ten of these unfortunate beings. "Master, have pity on us!" they cried out (Luke 17:13). Jesus healed all ten, but you will remember that only one came back to thank Him. "One of them, realizing that he had been cured, came back praising God in a loud voice.... Jesus took the occasion to say, 'Were not all ten made whole? Where are the other nine? Was there no one to return and give thanks to God except this foreigner?' He said to the man, 'Stand up and go your way; your faith has been your salvation.'" (Luke 17:15-19). How important it is to give thanks to God for blessings received!

Scripture is filled with such episodes, but the greatest manifestation of faith that the world has ever witnessed came from a man who started out as an enemy of Jesus—Saint Paul. "I am a Jew, born in Tarsus in Cilicia, but I was brought up in this city. Here I sat at the feet of Gamaliel and was educated strictly in the law of our fathers. I was a staunch defender of God, just as all of you are today. Furthermore I persecuted this new way to the point of death. I arrested and imprisoned both men and women." (Acts 22:3-4.)

It is traditionally accepted that the conversion of Paul (first known in the Bible as Saul) occurred following the shattering experience on the road to Damascus, when in a vision he heard the voice of Jesus saying, "Saul, Saul, why do you persecute me?" (Acts 9:4.) But it is my conviction that the seeds of his conversion were planted weeks or months before, when Saul (Paul) of Tarsus, the curse of Christians, stood by and watched a holy man die.

Jesus had warned His disciples that they would be reviled and persecuted in His name, in a long history of martrydom for those who followed in His steps. Their persecution was not long in coming. Within six years, Saint Stephen, first of an endless succession of martyrs, stood before a jeering crowd outside the walls of Jerusalem, where he was stoned to death for blasphemy, the same "crime" for which Jesus Himself was previously put to death.

Perhaps Saint Stephen could be considered the greatest of the martyrs, for it was he who set the example that thousands of other Christian martyrs were to follow. Had he wavered in his faith for even an instant, there is little doubt that early Christianity would not have witnessed the spectacles of so many other martyrs.

Stephen was one of the first deacons of the Jerusalem church, and Scripture tells us he was "filled with grace and power, who worked great wonders and signs among the people." (Acts 6:8.) Inevitably, he was brought before the high council; witnesses perjured themselves to swear falsely against him. Stephen's defense, told in Chapter Seven of Acts, is one of the most stirring episodes in the whole of Scripture. His final words accused them bluntly of putting Jesus, the Son of God, to death.

"Those who listened to his words were stung to the heart; they ground their teeth in anger at him. Stephen meanwhile, filled with the Holy Spirit, looked to the sky above and saw the glory of God, and Jesus standing at God's right hand. 'Look!' he exclaimed, 'I see an opening in the sky, and the Son of Man standing at God's right hand!' The onlookers were shouting aloud, holding their hands over their ears as they did so. Then they rushed at him as one man, dragged him out of the city, and began to stone him. The witnesses meanwhile were piling their cloaks at the feet of a young man named Saul. As Stephen was being stoned he could be heard praying, 'Lord Jesus, receive my spirit.' He fell to his knees and cried out in a loud voice, 'Lord, do not hold this sin against them.' And with that he died. Saul, for his part, concurred in the act of killing." (Acts 7:54-8:1.)

The death of Stephen unleashed a wave of persecution, with Saul in the forefront, against the sect of Christians, but subtly in the deeper consciousness of the man from Tarsus doubts began to form. He had been brought up to honor the old laws, one of the most honored of which was the law of retribution. Who ever heard of forgiving those who put you to death? Yet that is what Stephen did! And they say that is also what Jesus did when they nailed Him to the Cross.

As Saul (Paul) and his men made their rounds, bringing in Christians for judgment, he, Saul, became aware of something very strange indeed. There was no resistance; the Jesus followers of their day accepted their fate with equanimity, and day by day doubt deepened in the mind of Saul. Nothing in his entire life had prepared him for such attitudes, such serenity, and slowly but surely the persecutor felt the shame in his heart of persecution.

The thoughts came to him—if these people can accept death and persecution so nobly, where is the evil in them? If this be Christ-like, then there is virtue in this cult. And following him, day and night, were the haunting eyes of Stephen, forgiving those who caused his death. As he rode toward Damascus, to persecute more Christians, Saul unconsciously realized he was ready for conversion. The blood of Stephen, the martyr, won for the Church the conversion of Saul of Tarsus to Paul the apostle of the Gentiles. For each of us there comes such a time, and our free will is tested—to accept or not to accept.

Never is anyone so dedicated, so reverent, as a converted sinner, and so it was with Paul the Apostle. Almost single-handedly he guided the fortunes of the early Church, sustained by a living faith that stood as firm as the Rock of Gibraltar despite hardships and tribulations that could scarcely be endured . . . but with God's help he made it, because God and one is a majority.

To this great saint we owe perhaps the most easily understood of all definitions of faith: "Faith," he wrote, "is confident assurance concerning what we hope for, and conviction about things we do not see. . . . Through faith we perceive that the worlds were created by the word of God, and that what is visible came into being through the invisible." (Hebrews 11:1-3.)

God chose Saint Paul as His instrument for releasing the message of Jesus from within the confines of Israel and bringing it to the entire world. It is to him, more than to any other, that we owe the universality of Christianity, which was the mission of Jesus.

Today we need a return to the same faith, that of Stephen and Paul, for we have much more to do and a need to solve vastly greater problems. Stephen and Paul looked at Christianity through Jewish minds, Hebrew hearts, and a faith newly formed in the Messiah.

We look back on a history of two thousand years, the real proof of Christ's divinity, forgetting that our roots in Jesus are also Semitic. We may succeed in escaping ourselves, but we can never succeed in escaping God, which is to say that our origin, nature, and historic destiny tie in, no matter how little, to that of the Jews and Christ. We may not celebrate the Passover each year with our Jewish brethren, in which they commemorate the event of Moses, the Sea of Reeds, and their exodus from slavery in Egypt to freedom and dignity in

Palestine. But we who have been given faith and prayerful celebration may see a far greater Passover possible in our century!

The ancient people of God were enslaved throughout history far worse than any bondage under the Pharaohs. The edict of Rameses II against Hebrew children, like Herod's massacre of the Holy Innocents, was a modest crime compared to Hitler's concentration camps that shocked all the world. As if in shameful remorse for our own deep-felt complicity, we have played Moses in delivering his people from a far worse enemy than the Pharaoh.

Does it take any less faith to read the signs of our times than it did in the days of Moses or the years when Jesus Himself proclaimed, "The sky is red"?

Read the signs of the times! The sky is red from Hiroshima to Moscow, from Vietnam to Peking, from Cairo to Cuba.

We needed faith and courage to put men on the moon, the kind of faith and courage it took for the ancient Hebrews to follow Moses into the Sea of Reeds. Our "breakthrough" to overcome must now be with the same faith.

It is in the quiet solitude of an honest and contrite heart that we can meet the God in whom we believe, who is the way, the truth, and the life, the source of love and joy.

This is living by faith!

"Ask, and you will receive. Seek, and you will find. Knock, and it will be opened to you. For the one who asks, receives. The one who seeks, finds. The one who knocks, enters." (Matthew 7:7-8.)

The essence of prayer is, I think, openness to God; receptivity to God's action and God's will in whatever we do . . . that spiritual communication which places us in touch with God and reality.

—Jeane Dixon

12. The Transfiguration— Point of No Return

Why is there such an exodus from the institutional Church today?

Even priests, ministers, nuns, and bishops are leaving their chosen callings to seek their identities in other walks of life. Is it the influence of science, education, materialism, sex, leisure, communism, greater expectations from life, a loss of spiritual values . . . or what?

Including all of these things it is also much more.

Our past is catching up with us. We are becoming more open and honest as individuals and more true to the standards, good or evil, in which we believe. We are becoming less inconsistent and less hypocritical. We have seen the double standards of war, persecutions, oppressions, and hypocrisies bear their evil fruit in the betrayal of other human beings, and we have drawn inevitable conclusions. Our convictions have to shape up or be replaced!

An inventory of the spirit, a taking stock of things in a world where evils of every kind increase from day to day, is long overdue. A collective examination of conscience is in order. The magnitude and scope of all the historic evils to which we are heir have become so great that we can no longer gloss over them as the price of our "achievements," or ignore them in view of our "greatness." The amount of good and evil in the world is not constant, as Samuel Beckett says of tears and laughter; evil is becoming progressively greater in our world.

It is this awareness that weighs down the tender moral sensibilities of the very young, the very intelligent, and the very sensitive. It comes out in furious protests against war, poverty, politics, pollution, the oppression of one group by another. Unlike the great expectations and high ideals in other generations, many of today's youth are unfortunately without illusions. Their angry spokesmen see only the likelihood of more war, deeper poverty, an even worse environment, harsher government, less opportunity, and endless despair. Theirs is a bleak outlook.

Where is the biblical promise, "You will know the truth, and the truth will set you free"? (John 8:32.)

It seems a terribly irony. The great crime of the century, perhaps the greatest crime of all time, the blood of six million Jews, is on our conscience.

There are other, comparable calamities on our consciences, to be sure, but this incredible holocaust overshadows all the others. Nor have fifty-five million dead been enough to teach us the obvious lesson of "No More War!" Munich, Czechoslovakia, Pearl Harbor, and Vietnam are all catchwords of deception.

Most of the people of the world still live under some form of tyranny and domination, and those who do not seem equally unhappy. Finally, there is the threat of doom in the nuclear bomb polluting the human spirit, along with the failure of the United Nations to live up to its promise. Is it any wonder that there is loose talk everywhere of "revolution" and that so many people despair?

Is there any basis for hope?

Yes, there is. It is the last hope, the most difficult to understand, and really the only hope. It is the most ancient hope that brightens as all else fades, and it is full of the promise of a new and better day. It is the hope of true religion as embodied in the Transfiguration. It is as basic to life as food, air, and water, for "Where there is no vision the people perish."

The Transfiguration is the hope of discovering the truths of God as they exist within us, as Jesus discovered them when He exclaimed, "The reign of God is already in your midst." (Luke 17:21.) The mystery of the Transfiguration is to know Jesus for who He really is. Discovering the spirit of God within us is finally realizing what freedom is. It is the hope of achieving justice, peace, and dignity, and even, within limits, creating them for ourselves. In our search for God we find these things first, like the apostles, in the glorified Jesus— "glorified," that is, made transcendent, immortal, but also living on in us by the saving effect of His teaching, His forgiveness, and His love. Full participation in Christ's Transfiguration still lies ahead. In the attainment of it lies the key to our transfiguration from a hellish world to a happy, peaceful life.

One day as Jesus and His apostles walked along a dusty road leading northward and eastward out of Galilee, Jesus seemed withdrawn, lost in thought. During their journeys the Master often talked continually, recounting parables, answering questions, advising the apostles about their life together. But today He walked silently, and no one dared break the awesome silence.

The little group was actually in flight. Things had not been going well of late. Just a few days ago there had been a momentous encounter with a group of Pharisees and agents of Herod Antipas. They were out to "get" Jesus, and the more He discredited them the more menacing they became. As Jesus preached to a large crowd they shouted, "Teacher, we want to see you work some signs." (Matthew 12:38.)

It seemed like a fair challenge. This was the time-honored test of the true prophet—Elijah calling down fire from heaven, Moses striking the rock for water.

Jesus defied them with a far deeper interpretation of signs, the signs of the times in which they were living. "In the evening you say, 'Red sky at night, the day will be bright'; but in the morning, 'Sky red and gloomy, the day will be stormy.' If you know how to interpret the look of the sky, can you not read the signs of the times? An evil, faithless age is eager for a sign, but no sign will be given it, except that of Jonah." (Matthew 16:2-4.) Chapter Twelve of Saint Matthew adds, "Just as Jonah spent three days and three nights in the belly of the whale, so will the Son of Man spend three days and three nights in the bowels of the earth." (Matthew 12:40.)

Jesus was speaking of the turning point of all human history, His coming death and Resurrection. The signs of the times were all evident, as the prophets had foretold; yet no one understood Him! Realizing this, He suddenly exclaimed, "Who do people say that the Son of Man is?" They replied, "Some say John the Baptizer, others Elijah, still others Jeremiah or one of the prophets." (Matthew 16:13-14.)

" 'And you,' he said to them, 'who do you say that I am?' " (Matthew 16:15.)

For a moment there was deep silence, and then Peter spoke up. His reply has gone echoing down through the centuries: "You are the Messiah, . . . the Son of the living God!" (Matthew 16:16.)

For this moment the little group must have stopped walking! It was a startling moment, but normalcy returned, and no doubt they resumed walking; and Jesus went on: "Blest are you, Simon son of John! No mere man has revealed this to you, but my heavenly Father. I for my part declare to you, you are 'Rock,' and on this rock I will build my church, and the jaws of death shall not prevail against it." (Matthew 16:17-18.)

Scripture tells us that from that time on, Jesus spoke more and more of the old Messianic prophecies and how they must be fulfilled in Him: that He must go up to Jerusalem, be put to death and rise again the third day, as He had told the Pharisees.

Peter would not listen to such talk. "Master! God forbid that any such thing ever happen to you!"

"Get out of my sight, you satan!" said Jesus angrily. "You are trying to make me trip and fall. You are not judging by God's standards but by man's." (Matthew 16:22-23.)

Peter kept his peace, but the following words of Jesus' show that He was preoccupied with the events that were about to break like a hurricane over them all.

"If a man wishes to come after me," He said, "he must deny his very self, take up his cross, and begin to follow in my footsteps. Whoever would save his life will lose it, but whoever loses his life for my sake will find it. What profit would a man show if he were to gain the whole world and destroy himself in the process?" (Matthew 16:24-26.)

After this, the disappointment and chagrin Peter suffered in this rebuke by Jesus seemed to depress the other apostles as well. Who wanted to deny himself and look forward only to losing his life on a cross? Why not emulate the Maccabees and restore Israel to greatness through armed revolt? Both Peter and Judas and some of the other apostles were of the same mind about this. Judas Iscariot, seeing the inaction of Jesus and hearing about self-denial, must have been making up his mind about the betrayal at this time. The apostles were also engaging in debates about who was the greatest among them. Demoralization was setting in on all sides. It was a time like the present; something had to be done.

The Transfiguration was the answer of Jesus. It was the last great self-manifestation of His life, the experience of which would sustain the apostles through their trials and make the Resurrection finally credible.

One day, about a week after the harassment of the Pharisees and Peter's protest, as the group stopped to rest on the slopes of Mount Tabor, Jesus did not rest. A beckoning from the depths of His being drew Him toward the mountain, and as He heeded it, He took three of the apostles—Peter, James, and John—to accompany Him. As Saint Matthew tells the story (Matthew 17:1-9):

"Six days later Jesus took Peter, James, and his brother John and led them up on a high mountain by themselves. He was transfigured before their eyes. His face became as dazzling as the sun, his clothes as radiant as light. Suddenly Moses and Elijah appeared to them conversing with him.

"Then Peter said to Jesus, 'Lord, how good that we are here! With your permission I will erect three tents here, one for you, one for Moses, and one for Elijah.'

"He was still speaking when suddenly a bright cloud overshadowed them. Out of the cloud came a voice which said, 'This is my beloved Son on whom my favor rests. Listen to him.'

"When they heard this the disciples fell forward on the ground, overcome with fear.

"Jesus came toward them and laying his hand on them, said, 'Get up! Do not be afraid.' When they looked up they did not see anyone but Jesus.

"As they were coming down the mountainside Jesus commanded them, 'Do not tell anyone of the vision until the Son of Man rises from the dead.' "

So this was to be the inscrutable design of God. There would be no signs to the Pharisees except His Resurrection (Matthew 12:40), no miracles, no military uprising, no coming down from the Cross, no walking across Herod's bath.

The Transfiguration was a sign beyond miracles and prophecies. It is a sign for our time as well as it was for the time of Jesus, Moses, and Elijah. Its sign is a pulling aside momentarily of the veil of time to give us a glimpse of God's eternal view of history.

Just as we can now see the earth in the distant perspective of space as our beautiful blue planet all at once, so God can comprehend the entire drama of life in one eternal perspective, unlimited by concepts of space or time.

Jesus in the Transfiguration was the Jesus of the future, as He was for the apostles who saw Him in that moment of eternal glory; He was and is the Jesus of the Resurrection. Moses and Elijah are figures of the past which were then seen in their fulfillment in Christ. Like the Resurrection and the Second Coming, the future extends to eternity and so has no end. It is the reign of God already in our midst, yet always coming in greater fullness. It has its source in God, extends to us, and with us returns to God, who is all in all (1 Corinthians 15:28).

Jesus in the Transfiguration, like Jesus of the Resurrection, was timelessly detached from the troubles brewing for Him in Jerusalem—the acclaim and betrayal of the crowds, the desertion of His closest friends. The chief work of Moses and Elijah was completed on earth in preparation for all this; but it is still part of our own future along with the Transfiguration and Resurrection. The glory of Jesus with the Law and the prophets was being shaped for us in the matrix of history; it still is. There is even yet a greater distance to go than that we have already traveled ... but it is nearer than we realize.

The visionary experience is one we all need if we are to fulfill our potential in God's plan. How shall we ever get through our Good Fridays if we are not buoyed up by the occasional vision of our own particular destiny in

God? It must be a vision detached from the misfortunes and fortunes of life—for if we try to set up tents for our souls in the material world, the vision vanishes!

The Transfiguration occurred near the end of Christ's career. It marked the point of no return in a more final manner than the temptation in the desert or the entry into Jerusalem. Jesus could have quit at any time and returned to private life, but at every decisive point along the way He became more irrevocably committed to the destiny closing in on Him. His glorification on Tabor would have lost its significance if there had been no betrayal, no Crucifixion, no Resurrection, no prophecies to come, "that the Scriptures might be fulfilled." It is the resistance of the air that raises the wing!

In a very real sense our world has been transfigured since the coming of Jesus into it, just as all life has been undergoing a gradual transfiguration for the past thirty to thirty-five thousand years. Our view of the world, our knowledge of the universe and its elements, our capacities to live a godlike life proportionate to the speeds at which we travel, are as different from the ancient form of mind and matter as are the Transfigured Christ from the Jesus of the Way of the Cross.

What we need now is a comparable transfiguration of the spirit!

The Transfiguration now means Jesus risen and returning in great power and majesty with Moses on the one hand and Elijah on the other. It means the Messiah showing us who He really is in glory, as He showed His closest apostles. It means our acceptance of Him as the fulfillment of the Law and the prophets, the Christ, the Son of God acclaimed by Peter, the expected of the nations, the alpha and omega who was, who is, and who is to come.

This is the vision which the many have failed to grasp. This is the vision which has vanished in a maze of church buildings, lobbies, surface reforms, personality clashes, and theological wrangling. This is also the reason why bishops, priests, and people are leaving the institutional churches in unprecedented numbers because they have looked at the face of the sky and have failed to perceive the signs of the times!

The vision of the Transfiguration is the essence of the modern religious message: the Law, the prophets, the return of Jesus to Jerusalem! The long Palm Sunday period of Christianity is about spent; the crowds are deserting Him now, and even His disciples are having their doubts. The new Good Friday is just ahead—and then the glorious new Easter!

I see them all coming together again in the new, revitalized religion of the future, when there shall be but one fold and one shepherd. The fold will be worldwide and the shepherd will be Jesus. His throne shall be as the prophets all agree on a new Mount Zion, in a new Jerusalem. This will be the new age of Moses and Elijah fulfilled in the Messiah; an age, like the Resurrection, which will come about after the deluge of suffering that will end the present era.

This new era will begin early in the next century. I cannot be more definite about it than that because the more distant events are, the less distinct they appear. It is much like approaching a tableau in space: the closer you get, the more clearly you see it.

As we approach this crisis of history, the faith of many will fail and the charity of many more will completely disappear. But those who hold firm to the vision of the Transfiguration will not fail in either! They will understand the revolution taking place as men lose faith in their institutions and one another, only to find that the Law and the prophets are eternal, that Jesus comes again so that Jerusalem may rise from its ruins and rebuild the temple of the spirit to replace the former one as the spiritual capital of humanity.

The Transfiguration means all these things and more.

It means, finally, the resolution of the identity problem of each of us. We are called by God to be transfigured in the secret inner shrine of our own heart, the holy of holies of our inmost soul, where we are accessible only to ourselves and to God. It is here that the spirit of Jesus must be welcomed before He can return to the new Jerusalem!

The Transfiguration of our time and the new age to come can be celebrated in the words of David:

> I rejoiced because they said to me,
> "We will go up to the house of the Lord."
> And now we have set foot
> within your gates, O Jerusalem—
> Jerusalem, built as a city
> with compact unity.
>
> To it the tribes go up,
> the tribes of the Lord,
> According to the decree for Israel,
> to give thanks to the name of the Lord.
> In it are set up judgment seats,
> seats for the house of David.
>
> Pray for the peace of Jerusalem!
> May those who love you prosper!
> May peace be within your walls,
> prosperity in your buildings.
> Because of my relatives and friends
> I will say, "Peace be within you!"
> Because of the house of the Lord, our God,
> I will pray for your good.
>
> —Psalm 122

"Avoid greed in all its forms. A man may be wealthy, but his possessions do not guarantee him life." (Luke 12:15.)

Like Judas, we have betrayed our religion, our institutions, our culture and ourselves. Free living has proved too much for us! But unlike Judas, we must not despise and try to destroy ourselves, but seek and accept the forgiveness of God.

—Jeane Dixon

13. A Prayer for Judas Iscariot—and for Us!

The whole life of Jesus Christ was a repudiation of injustice and cruelty. It was really more than that, it was also a plea for justice and love. As the Gospel tells it, He went about doing good. He cured the sick, forgave the erring, even demanded that His disciples love their enemies. He was Himself a victim of perfidy and betrayal. How His followers have treated friend and enemy alike down through the centuries has been the paradox of Christian history.

The long list of religious wars, persecutions, and oppressions committed in the name of Christ and His religion have been one of the scandals of Western society. Toynbee makes a special point of it in his study of history and makes it the subject of a special study: *The World and the West*. The lessons of Jesus are so perfect; our practice so contradictory! Even in this late time the people of Northern Ireland puzzle us by bombing and killing one another in the name of the gentle Jesus, who told them to love one another. Why can they not see that their actions are a denial of their faith? Why have we been so afflicted with the same schizophrenia throughout Christian history? How is it that we still point out the sliver in our brother's eye, but refuse to believe that there is a beam in our own?

There seems to be something to Lord Acton's adage

about the corruption of absolute power. No sooner did Christian nations become powerful than they began warring with those of other faiths and with one another. The Conquistadores who followed Columbus to the New World behaved no better and no worse than the Europeans who went on Crusades to the Old World of the East, pillaging everything along the way, and on expeditions to Africa, India, and China, where they oppressed the peoples they found there. So often the religious missionary was followed by the soldier, the merchant, and the civil administrator, and people who at first welcomed conversion, all too sadly found themselves in colonial bondage rather than in religious freedom.

The success of the first Jesuit missionaries in China in the sixteenth century held great promise for the world; but it was not long before the old patterns of abuse and exploitation replaced the Gospel message, so that Western pioneers were expelled from Japan in the seventeenth century and from China in the eighteenth. But their successors came back in the nineteenth century and threatened the East by force with weapons more terrible and deadly than ever. Rather than risk conquest, the Japanese decided to learn for themselves how to make and use these new weapons, which eventually led to Pearl Harbor, with disastrous consequences.

In the New World, the same woeful scenes were taking place. From Cotton Mather in Massachusetts to Pizarro in South America, the natives of the forest were considered encumbrances who had to be removed or exterminated. It is not only their liquidation that outrages our sense of justice, but the means by which it was carried out. When the Jesuit missionaries from their South American headquarters protested to the crown against the barbarism of the conquerors, they were simply expelled from the country! The most eloquent witness to the colonization of Mexico and Latin America, William H. Prescott, tells in *The Conquest of Peru* how an Inca chief was held for ransom in gold and then clubbed to death when the ransom was paid. An Aztec chief, threatened with death should he refuse to accept Christianity, said to his captors: "This heaven you speak of, will you go there, too?" When assured that they would, he declared: "Then I accept your death, for I would not wish to be in a place where cruel men like you will also be."

From the Crusades to the Nazis, while the Jews have been the worst sufferers, Christians have been victimized with the same regularity, Catholics and Protestants alike. Simon de Montfort, besieging the city of Beziers in the anti-Albigensian crusade, was typical. Within the city were "true believers" and "heretics" alike. "How," asked the Papal Legate, "can my soldiers tell which are heretics and which are believers in the true Church?"

"Kill them all," came Simon's icy answer. "God will know His own!"

Four centuries later, Cromwell was to be no less ruthless on the other side. Fifteen thousand men, women, and children had been butchered by de Montfort at Beziers; at Drogheda, a city of about the same size, Cromwell duplicated the massacre, slaughtering its inhabitants *en masse*. "It hath pleased God to bless our endeavors," he said, trying to justify these actions.

Thus did the followers of Jesus Christ slay one another by the thousands in His name!

Probably the worst single case of persecution was suffered by Joan of Arc, a Christian saint who was martyred, like Jesus, after having been betrayed by her own people. She was condemned by a church court, denounced by her own bishop, and burned at the stake, paralleling closely the trial and Crucifixion of Jesus. She is now her country's patron saint, and George Bernard Shaw immortally dramatized her life in his tragedy *Saint Joan*. He asks: *"Must then Christ perish in every age to save those who have no imagination?"*

And then how can we say that Judas Iscariot alone was the betrayer of Christ!

Today the betrayal of Jesus takes place at a different level. Cracker-barrel theologies, situation morality, do-it-yourself liturgy, are all piecemeal betrayals of religious faith. Advocates of The Secular City and a Feast of Fools do more than alcoholism and drug abuse combined to destroy society, because they strike at its very roots! Advocates of the city without spirituality erode religion to the vanishing point. They undermine the very foundations of the temple. The whole collection of new religious symbols of a reawakened charity in the underground Church are signs of a deep humanitarianism fostered by religion, but they are not religion. On the surface these symbolic acts seem so much like our long-lost faith that it is easy for us to mistake their upsurge as a return of the real thing. Humanitarianism goes back at least to John the Baptist and shows that there is a genuine religious heritage in the society that is generous. It is certainly a good thing in its own right. But it would be as disastrous a mistake to let humanitarianism take over religion as it would be to give Judas the status of Christ.

At the practical level Judas has even more to teach us. Today we are selling our souls for silver and gold and the passing pleasures that go with them. Corporations justify their reasons for bringing in ever higher and higher profits, labor unions put their own gains ahead of public interest, growing numbers of people dodge work for welfare payments. Everyone is so intent upon doing his own thing, going his own way, making his own pile, that the good of the whole is threatened. The inflation of our currency, the pollution of the environment, the divisions among our people are traceable to the same greedy self-centeredness which turned Judas from a friend into a devil. It could happen to anyone. Little by little we betray ourselves into greater self-deceptions when we place gold before God, money ahead of principle. I see America as well as some other countries going down this path of materialism at the sacrifice of their inner spiritual being and future success and peace for all.

Will Durant writes: "Industry and trade are the substances of economic life. But in the midst of wealth, poverty increases, for the same variety and freedom of exchange that enables the clever to make money, allows the simple to lose it faster than before. Under the new economy, the poor are relatively poorer than in the days of serfdom."

He is writing not about the twentieth century but about ancient Greece!

A famous American has said that if we refuse to learn the lessons of history, we condemn ourselves to relive them.

Every person is endowed by his or her Creator with certain "inalienable rights, among which are life, liberty and the pursuit of happiness." But let us never forget that each person is also endowed by the Creator with *certain inalienable responsibilities,* among which are certain life missions and purposes to be accomplished. Such purposes and missions, the most serious things in any life, must be placed before profit, pride, or pleasure. The Creator endows each individual with the gifts and talents necessary to accomplish his or her mission. Upon their faithful use depends the successful pursuit of happiness or the hellish nightmare of failure for one's self.

This was the failure of Judas, as it is our failure today, in large numbers.

Judas, instead of using his very considerable talents as an apostle, tried to turn them to his own advantage. This early type of opportunist saw in Jesus a great asset who could sway crowds and work miracles, the greatest rabbi of the time, who confounded the scribes and Pharisees at every turn and escaped from hostile mobs at will! Even Peter thought nothing could happen to Jesus. The thirty pieces of silver Judas pocketed were only a small payoff for the beginning of an investment that would make a fortune. Thirty pieces of silver, just to point out Jesus!

How differently it all turned out. The last thing Judas expected was what actually happened, his own death and the disaster on Calvary.

It will be no different for us, now or ever!

Following the Last Supper, Jesus and three of His apostles made their way to the Garden of Olives, prepared to spend the night in prayer. Jesus knew that it was the last night of His earthly life; He had told His friends, saying He would not drink the wine of the covenant until they were together again in the Kingdom of God. He knew He would be denied by one friend, betrayed by another, deserted in death by nearly all. "My heart is nearly broken with sorrow," He told them (Matthew 26:38). "Sit down here while I pray." (Mark 14:32.)

As Saint Matthew tells the story of what happened (Matthew 26:39-50):

"He advanced a little and fell prostrate in prayer. 'My Father, if it is possible, let this cup pass me by. Still, let it be as you would have it, not as I.'

"When he returned to his disciples, he found them asleep. He said to Peter, 'So you could not stay awake with me for even an hour? Be on guard, and pray that you may not undergo the test. The spirit is willing but nature is weak.'

"Withdrawing a second time, he began to pray: 'My Father, if this cannot pass me by without my drinking it, your will be done!'

"Once more, on his return, he found them asleep; they could not keep their eyes open.

"He left them again, withdrew somewhat, and began to pray a third time, saying the same words as before. Finally he returned to his disciples and said to them:

'Sleep on now. Enjoy your rest! The hour is on us when the Son of Man is to be handed over to the power of evil men. Get up! Let us be on our way! See, my betrayer is here.'

"While he was still speaking, Judas, one of the Twelve, arrived accompanied by a great crowd with swords and clubs. They had been sent by the chief priests and elders of the people.

"His betrayer had arranged to give them a signal, saying, 'The man I shall embrace is the one; take hold of him.'

"He immediately went over to Jesus, said to him, 'Peace, Rabbi,' and embraced him.

"Jesus answered, 'Friend, do what you are here for!'

"At that moment they stepped forward to lay hands on Jesus, and arrested him."

"All this has happened in fulfillment of the writings of the prophets." (Matthew 26:56.)

Almost immediately, when Judas saw things going wrong, he regretted it. Chapter Twenty-seven of Saint Matthew states:

"Then Judas, who had handed him over, seeing that Jesus had been condemned, began to regret his action deeply. He took the thirty pieces of silver back to the chief priests and elders and said, 'I did wrong to deliver up an innocent man!' They retorted, 'What is that to us? It is your affair!'

"So Judas flung the money into the temple and left. He went off and hanged himself."

Judas, seeing the evil result of his private schemes, regretted it. I pray, therefore, that he was forgiven. In the Acts of the Apostles the details of his death are recounted; the rope or branch broke in the hanging and Judas fell to the ground. He was found dead. The moment of that fall was sufficient for God's mercy. I believe it happened just that way.

Jesus prayed on the Cross for the forgiveness of His executioners; surely Judas must have been included. Jesus also prayed at the Last Supper, "As long as I was with them, I guarded them with your name which you gave me. I kept careful watch, and not one of them was lost, none but him who was destined to be lost—in fulfillment of Scripture."

Judas, indeed, was the one "destined to be lost," but he too could surely have been forgiven by the goodness and mercy of Jesus if he were truly repentant. What a tragedy to become the victim of greed for money and thus lose the riches of God's mercy. That is what hell is!

Jesus' lesson of mercy and forgiveness is the one most needed today if we are to begin to build a world of peace, of freedom, and of dignity.

Can the Jews forgive the Nazis? Can blacks and whites be reconciled in understanding? Can rich and poor, young and old, Communists and anti-Communists come to respect each other in peace and love?

Is this asking too much? No!!! It is the requirement for the survival of mankind.

We should not make forgiveness and brotherhood more difficult than they are. Beginnings have already been made. Have we not had an abundance of success as a united people with our portion of the world? I see this dramatized in the diversity of the crowds that go daily to visit the "Eternal Flame" marking the late President Kennedy's gravesite. It has become a kind of national shrine. Pilgrims stream there by the thousands each day, because they sense the inevitability in that President's call to destiny, something of the same opportunity God gives everyone in America. Americans forgive their enemies more readily than other nations, not because they have suffered less, but because they are a compassionate nation, composed of many formerly warring peoples. I feel sure the late President forgave Lee Harvey Oswald, not because his family suffered less but because he understood, at last, his mission in the plan of God.

How do I know?

On that dark day of November 25, 1963, as the Kennedy cortege made its sad way from the church to the cemetery, I had a vision of the late President dancing on his coffin before the trumpets of the Lord, like King David before the Ark of the Covenant. As the funeral procession made its solemn way to Arlington, I felt him smiling peacefully down upon the world because his spirit had found joy in the presence of God. This was the fulfillment of the promise of salvation, and he forgot the tragedy that bore him there.

As Jesus forgave Judas, John Kennedy forgave Oswald, for when we understand our destiny in the Kingdom of God, nothing is impossible for us.

On that incredible day of November 25, 1963, all the world was one under God in peace, love, and understanding! It has never been so united, before or since! That was the day that mercy and forgiveness reigned supreme in the hearts of men, and it held great promise for the future.

We must somehow achieve that spirit again and make it endure.

The way we can achieve this enduring spirit is not only through martyrdom and suffering but the way that Jesus taught, to love our enemies and do good to those who hate us. We must use our God-given talents for the benefit of each other ... to build rather than destroy one another! As someone said when asked how he treated his enemies: "I treat them well and turn them into friends."

Like Judas we have betrayed our religion, our institutions, our culture, and ourselves. We have made "high living" our God just as Judas tried to do. If we are to have this better world that we envision we must radically change our daily habits and learn to fulfill our individual roles as foreordained by God for the benefit of all mankind.

Without such changing and learning we will *all come* to a sad end, perhaps even worse than Judas.

A prayer for Judas is a prayer for ourselves.

"I am the light of the world. No follower of mine shall ever walk in darkness." (John 8:12.)

The faith of the future will be as different from the religion of the past as the risen Jesus was from the gentle Galilean rabbi put to death by the chief priests and the Romans. Even His friends did not recognize Him in the Resurrection! We shall witness a revitalized faith at the end of our era that will restore our religious values to their rightful place; but first we must pass under the redeeming Sign of the Cross.

—Jeane Dixon

14. "I Am the Resurrection and the Life"

The hours dragged by on Calvary, on that long-ago day of infamy, and the tortured figure on the Cross was near His end. His head fell forward, and the group of onlookers faithful to Jesus knew that the unbelievable ordeal was over. Those who loved Him wept unashamedly. They were numb from pain, surprise, and disbelief. Why had this week, which had begun so gloriously with the crowds excitedly chanting "hosannas" to the Son of David, ended so disastrously at this "Place of the Skull," where saints, felons, and slaves alike were executed? The ugly mob, the jeering high priests, Pharisees and scribes, and the cynical soldiery were gone; through all the scorn and torment the spirit of Jesus remained indomitable: "Father, forgive them; they do not know what they are doing." (Luke 23:34.)

"Forgive them." Simple words that symbolize the life of Jesus and His sacred mission, for as Saint John says, "God did not send the Son into the world to condemn the world, but that the world might be saved through him." (John 3:17.) Jesus was the ombudsman of man.

And now He was gone.

Casually the soldiers moved off, one carrying the cloak of Jesus. Joseph of Arimathea, distinguished in history by this act of kindness, hastened to Pilate to beg the body for burial. Scripture tells us that Pilate was surprised to learn that Jesus was already dead (Mark 15:44), for most crucified men lingered on for days. The compassionate request was speedily granted.

Returning to the Cross, Joseph and his helpers went about the delicate task of removing the sacred body. Ever so reverently, the hands and feet were freed of the spikes and the lifeless form was carefully lowered onto a marble slab for its last anointing.

We can imagine the little group making its way to the tomb, following the traditional ceremony, and then dispersing into the darkest of nights.

The site of that apocalyptic scene may still be visited today. Crowds stand in line daily at the Church of the Holy Sepulchre to inspect in solemn silence the mound on which the Cross stood, the slab of the anointing, and the final place of burial.

The Death of Jesus!

The curtain falls on the greatest cosmic drama of all time.

It is finished!

But that was not the end—only a new beginning! With the death of Jesus on Golgotha, a new era dawned for humanity. He bequeathed us a new understanding of God's love. With Him died the old idea of sacrifice and atonement in the Law, "eye for eye, tooth for tooth, hand for hand" (Exodus 21:24). With Jesus a new ideal of mercy and forgiveness took root. "It is mercy I desire and not sacrifice," He had said to his followers, citing the Scripture (Matthew 9:13).

How deeply He lived this new ideal came out in His last hours as He prayed from the Cross: "Father, forgive them; they do not know what they are doing." (Luke 23:34.)

Jesus of Nazareth kindled a light that would illuminate the Christian world forever. Ernest Renan, an agnostic, after describing the Crucifixion, wrote: "A thousand times more living, a thousand times more loved since thy death than during the days of thy pilgrimage here below, thou wilt become to such a degree the corner-stone of humanity, that to tear thy name from this world would be to shake it to its foundations. Between thee and God, men will no longer distinguish. Complete conquerer of death, take possession of thy kingdom, whither, by the royal road thou hast traced, ages of adorers will follow thee."

"Complete conqueror of death," Renan calls Jesus. The Resurrection has been the subject of endless controversy, but Renan, an unbeliever, incredibly makes the essential point. The miracles of Jesus from Cana to Golgotha served to distinguish Him from other itinerant preachers and set Him as a man apart, identified as the great prophet, the Messiah, and, most importantly, as the Son of God.

The Resurrection was God's way of immortalizing that distinction and placing the final seal of heaven's approval on the life of Christ. "This is my beloved Son on whom my favor rests. Listen to him." (Matthew 17:5.)

It was the climax of a long series of biblical signs and wonders: Moses turning his rod into a serpent; the miraculous Red Sea passage; the avenging angel of the Passover; water struck from the rock in the desert; Joshua crossing the Jordan and later taking the city of Jericho; the resplendent Star of Bethlehem and the angelic host of that first Christmas night; the many miracles that attended the ministry of Jesus wherever He went.

The Resurrection was also God's way of electrifying the apostles, who were demoralized after Good Friday, into a magnetic society again.

We hear of the risen Christ almost immediately. As

Saint Mark tells the story in Chapter Sixteen: "When the Sabbath was over, Mary Magdalene, Mary the mother of James, and Salome bought perfumed oils with which they intended to go and anoint Jesus. Very early, just after sunrise, on the first day of the week they came to the tomb. They were saying to one another, 'Who will roll back the stone for us from the entrance to the tomb?' When they looked, they found that the stone had been rolled back. (It was a huge one.)

"On entering the tomb they saw a young man sitting at the right, dressed in a white robe. This frightened them thoroughly, but he reassured them:

" 'You need not be amazed! You are looking for Jesus of Nazareth, the one who was crucified. He has been raised up; he is not here. See the place where they laid him.

" 'Go now and tell his disciples and Peter, "He is going ahead of you to Galilee, where you will see him just as he told you." ' "

And they did see Him, time after time. But the first to see Him again was Mary Magdalene. "Mary stood weeping beside the tomb. Even as she wept, she stooped to peer inside, and there she saw two angels in dazzling robes. One was seated at the head and the other at the foot of the place where Jesus' body had lain. 'Woman,' they asked her, 'why are you weeping?' She answered them, 'Because the Lord has been taken away, and I do not know where they have put him.' She had no sooner said this than she turned around and caught sight of Jesus standing there. But she did not know him. 'Woman,' he asked her, 'why are you weeping? Who is it you are looking for?' She supposed he was the gardener, so she said, 'Sir, if you are the one who carried him off, tell me where you have laid him and I will take him away.'

"Jesus said to her, 'Mary!' She turned to him and said [in Hebrew], *Rabbouni!* (meaning 'Teacher'). Jesus then said: 'Do not cling to me, for I have not yet ascended to the Father.' " (John 20:11-17.)

The touching scene was full of religious significance. Mary Magdalene sought to honor her Lord in death; instead, to her amazement, she found Him alive! But she did not recognize Him until He addressed her by name. Jesus was the same person, but somehow different, in some way changed. In the Resurrection He had shed His temporal human form to be, henceforth, an eternal divine presence rather than the once familiar corporeal entity of everyday experience. This explains Mary's failure to recognize Him as He stood before her, and also that of the two disciples on the road to Emmaus, who did not know Him until they recognized Him in "the breaking of the bread." It also explains His admonition to Mary not to cling to Him—which is otherwise not clear.

I find all this familiar and readily understandable because of my own mystical experiences. As others, I too have seen Jesus and listened to His voice. These experiences are almost impossible to describe, and others who have had them say the same thing.

Mary Magdalene and later the apostles saw in the risen Jesus a regenerated personality. Divinity has no "look" and no "sound," as we understand the terms, and can be characterized only as an overpowering spiritual presence, an awareness of something infinite beyond comprehension. It was this new dimension of the Resurrection in Jesus that explains why Mary of Magdala, who had known Jesus like a brother, failed to recognize Him as He stood before her in the resurrected state. The same experience awaited the doubter, Thomas the Apostle, until he put his fingers into the wounded hands and his hand in the side of Jesus.

After reading of the appearance of Jesus to Mary of Magdala and the other women, we must follow from gospel to gospel to learn the sequence of events during the next few weeks. There are so many gaps in the gospel narrative that many scholars believe much, or at least some, of the original records of His movements must have been lost. Jesus appeared and then just as suddenly vanished. He was seen by one, then two or three witnesses ... then by five hundred at a time. The apostles were understandably upset in the face of happenings beyond their comprehension, and they fought for some kind of equilibrium.

Several of the apostles went back to Galilee after the Crucifixion and Resurrection, and it was there, on the shores of the lake where they had spent so much time together, that they also encountered the risen Jesus. Peter and his companions had been fishing with no success. As day was breaking, Jesus appeared on the beach, but in the emerging pattern of all the appearances of the resurrected Jesus, none of them recognized Him.

"Just after daybreak Jesus was standing on the shore, though none of the disciples knew it was Jesus.

"He said to them, 'Children, have you caught anything to eat?'

" 'Not a thing,' they answered.

" 'Cast your net off to the starboard side,' he suggested, 'and you will find something.' So they made a cast, and took so many fish they could not haul the net in.

"Then the disciple Jesus loved cried out to Peter, 'It is the Lord!' On hearing it was the Lord, Simon Peter threw on some clothes—he was stripped—and jumped into the water.

"Meanwhile the other disciples came in the boat, towing the net full of fish. Actually they were not far from land—no more than a hundred yards.

"When they landed, they saw a charcoal fire there with fish laid on it and some bread.

" 'Bring some of the fish you just caught,' Jesus told them.

"Simon Peter went aboard and hauled ashore the net loaded with sizable fish—one hundred fifty-three of them! In spite of the great number, the net was not torn.

" 'Come and eat your meal,' Jesus told them. Not one of the disciples presumed to inquire, 'Who are you?' for they knew it was the Lord.

"Jesus came over, and took the bread and gave it to them, and did the same with the fish.

"This marked the third time that Jesus appeared to the disciples after being raised from the dead.

"When they had eaten their meal, Jesus said to Simon Peter, 'Simon, son of John, do you love me more than these?' 'Yes, Lord,' he said, 'you know that I love you.' At which Jesus said, 'Feed my lambs.'

"A second time he put his question, 'Simon, son of John, do you love me?' 'Yes, Lord,' Peter said, 'you know that I love you.' Jesus replied, 'Tend my sheep.'

"A third time Jesus asked him, 'Simon, son of John, do you love me?' Peter was hurt because he had asked a third time, 'Do you love me?' So he said to him: 'Lord, you know everything. You know well that I love you.' Jesus said to him, 'Feed my sheep.' " (John 21:4-17.)

Matthew narrates the final meeting of Jesus with His apostles. His gospel closes with this climax: "Jesus came forward and addressed them in these words: 'Full authority has been given to me both in heaven and on earth; go, therefore, and make disciples of all the nations.

" 'Baptize them in the name "of the Father, and of the Son, and of the Holy Spirit." Teach them to carry out everything I have commanded you. And know that I am with you always, until the end of the world!' " (Matthew 28:18-20.)

The rest is history. A short time later, Peter was back in Jerusalem, taking up where the Master had left off, and soon after that he was put in prison for creating a disturbance. It was not long before Paul came on the scene. The new world faith was on its way.

Three hundred years later this faith was the official religion of the empire which had executed its Founder and crushed His nation. Two hundred years after that the empire itself was extinct—along with every other empire that had ever ruled Israel!

In the ensuing centuries the nations of Europe grew to power, and now they themselves are in decline. Three great super-powers overshadow the world of today and its future. Back into this sinful world Jesus will come again, in a way so divinely powerful that everyone will be completely amazed.

Jesus Himself said, "Men will see the Son of Man coming in the clouds with great power and glory" (Mark 13:26). Speaking thus of His second coming, Jesus took the figure from Chapter Seven of the Book of Daniel and applied it to Himself:

> I saw one like a son of man coming,
>   on the clouds of heaven;
> When he reached the Ancient One
>   and was presented before him,
> He received dominion, glory, and kingship;
>   nations and peoples of every
>   language serve him.
> His dominion is an everlasting dominion
>   that shall not be taken away,
>   his kingship shall not be destroyed."
>   —Daniel 7:13-14

Biblical scholars generally agree that the son of man in Daniel was a figure for the theocratic kingdom. Applying the figure to Himself, Jesus was saying that He would return in all power and glory with the New Israel, the People of God. The two would go together. The image of coming in great power and majesty on the clouds of heaven and the reality it foretells has already begun to take form. Ancient Israel will have been resurrected from the tomb of history. From its ordeal of persecution to its growth as a nation that we see at the crossroads of the world in the Middle East today, we are reminded, though less strikingly, of the growth of Christianity from the catacombs of Rome to the Empire of Constantine. Through the centuries of dispersion Israel makes its return to the family of believers appropriate to the figure in the Book of Daniel, coming on the clouds of heaven, with great power and glory. The accession of Jesus to His rightful place in the New Israel, His acknowledgement by the Israelites as the Son of Man, will be no less so. (Romans 11:25-32.)

It will be then that all the peoples of the world will stream to the Temple of the Lord, up to the Holy Mountain where "all the ends of the earth will behold the salvation of our God" (Isaiah 52:10).

After His Resurrection, Jesus did not go back to Jerusalem to take up the old quarrels with the scribes and Pharisees; He left the pettiness of man buried in the tomb. In His resurrected being He began his true mission: to send His apostles to all nations. The resurrected Israel likewise has a spiritual mission, which will transcend all the ancient quarrels and threats of empires long dead. It must get on with the business of building the temple anew, preparing the way for the Messiah, bringing God to man and man to God. It must prepare us for the days of which Isaiah spoke:

> In days to come,
> The mountain of the Lord's house
>   shall be established
>   as the highest mountain
>   and raised above the hills.
> All nations shall stream toward it;
>   many peoples shall come and say:
> "Come, let us climb the Lord's mountain,

to the house of the God of Jacob,
That he may instruct us in his ways,
    and we may walk in his paths."
For from Zion shall go forth instruction,
    and the word of the Lord from Jerusalem.
He shall judge among the nations,
    and impose terms on many peoples.
They shall beat their swords into plowshares
    and their spears into pruning hooks;
One nation shall not raise the sword
    against another,
    nor shall they train for war again.
O house of Jacob, come,
    let us walk in the light of the Lord!

—Isaiah 2:2-5

He is the Resurrection and the Life.

We will have passed under the redeeming Sign of the Cross!

"As he was making his way out of the temple area, one of his disciples said to him, 'Teacher, look at the huge blocks of stone and the enormous buildings!' Jesus said to him, 'You see these great buildings? Not one stone will be left upon another—all will be torn down.'

While he was seated on the Mount of Olives facing the temple, Peter, James, John, and Andrew began to question him privately. 'Tell us, when will this occur? What will be the sign that all this is coming to an end?'

Jesus began his discourse 'Be on your guard. Let no one mislead you. Any number will come attempting to impersonate me. "I am he," they will claim, and will lead many astray. When you hear about wars and threats of war, do not yield to panic. Such things are bound to happen, but this is not yet the end. Nation will rise against nation, one kingdom against another. There will be earthquakes in various places and there will be famine. This is but the onset of the pains of labor. Be constantly on your guard.' " (Mark 13:1–9.)

The prophets of old have predicted the Second Coming of Christ but not until the Antichrist has led the world to Armageddon. These prophecies will all be fulfilled.

—Jeane Dixon

15. Destiny: The Prophets and Our Times

During the past third of a century man has learned more, achieved more, and attempted more than in all the periods of his past history combined. Even the sky is no longer the limit as we dream of going to planets and worlds beyond our present horizons in the unknown universe. In fact, we begin to anticipate the disappearance of all horizons. We are on the brink of even greater discoveries than any we now contemplate. But there is a limit to what science can do and there must be control over the direction it takes—or we will destroy ourselves even quicker and more completely than we have feared with the devices of death we have already contrived.

Alvin Toffler has made the most dramatic study of all

the overlapping revolutions that engulf us, from population increase to the new and growing capacity for instant death to all life on earth. Until yesterday, the familiar pattern goes, humanity did not exist in any great numbers. It took about fifty thousand years for our species to increase and multiply to the extent of one billion, but in the past century or so we doubled and then trebled that figure. Not only that; the more the population increases, the faster it grows. As a result, soon the population of the world could be doubling every fifteen years, other factors remaining constant.

Advances in other fields have been equally dramatic. For fifty thousand years man could travel no faster than his feet or an animal could carry or pull him, or a small boat could transport him. It was not until the last century, with the aid of steam power, that man reached speeds common today in the life of everyone. Consequently, through all these thousands of years, few men strayed very far from home, and such rare long trips as took place were made for purposes of discovery or migration. They took months or years, and their results were not apparent for centuries. Today's voyages of discovery accelerate quickly to 18,500 miles per hour and they go to the moon. Their results are analyzed and computed at once, pointing to stellar distances and more radical concepts of speed to come.

Every other phase of human life is undergoing a comparable "accelerative thrust" of change. Even in publishing, some books are half absolete before distribution, because things change so much between the time the book is written and the time it is published. Many new weapons are obsolete before they are deployed or put into the hands of troops. Wherever you turn—business, education, family life, politics, the law, cybernetics, science, religion, medicine, the arts—everything is in a state of ferment and revolutionary change. Toffler says we are reaching a critical point in our ever-quickening rate of change and that we must deliberately step into the maze of threatening chaos and slow it down. Otherwise humanity will face the crisis of an "adaptational breakdown," which may already have begun as some people, finding they cannot adapt to such rapidity of change, react against the phenomenon of change itself. All of us are beginning to be afflicted with this same disease of rootlessness, restlessness, impermanence, and transience, which Toffler calls "future shock."

I have warned repeatedly of another kind of "future shock" with the same roots but with more disastrous consequences. Scientific futurists like Alvin Toffler are in reality social engineers and they necessarily deal in speculations of sociological and psychological theory when they speak of cultural change. My approach is basically different; it is religious. Due to no merit of my own, it is the same gift that is the basis of prophecy in both the Old and New Testaments, making it possible to be definite to a degree unknown to scientific futurists and to dispense with the reservations they quite rightfully and necessarily claim.

During the last decade I repeatedly sounded warnings to the Kennedy and Johnson administrations of the Russian perfection of their "monster bombs" and delivery systems. In 1961 I saw the Russians test and complete their masterpiece, the monster bomb; it was later revealed to me in terms of megatons. In 1962 I saw the Russians perfect an anti-missile missile. In rapid succession I saw an anti-satellite atomic burst, then the perfection of the MIRV (Multiple Independent Reentry Vehicle), which I called the "submarine of the sky." It had nine missiles programmed to strike at nine of our cities simultaneously. Next came the FOBS (Fractional Orbital Bombardment System), followed by a full orbital bombardment system in 1970. I warned the Russians that their space platform, which in reality was a platform from which they could aim and fire, would fail and end in tragedy. Now I see the Russians in the final stages of completing the "cosmos" series of anti-satellite missiles.

All my warnings are to no avail. Even when I described in detail the effects of electromagnetic emissions from the monster bombs—how radios, electrical circuitry, telephones, lights, and even our Minuteman missiles would be knocked out or fused beyond repair—no one paid attention! Instead of heeding my warnings that we should catch up with the Soviets, my warnings were questioned.

I mention these events because such systems will play an important part in fulfilling the prophecy of Armageddon.

The first half of this decade will prove important in this chain of events. President Nixon will long be remembered for his courage in removing the dollar from the grasp of the greedy gold manipulators, who used this procedure for their own ends. The United States will continue to improve its relations with Communist China. Trade will increase and we will assist in industrializing this great new Communist state. This the U.S.S.R. refused to do. I saw the Russians telling the Chinese that they (the Soviets) have the industrial might to destroy the United States, and to help industrialize China would set their timetable back fifty years.

I see a cloud over travel, and political upheavals and scandals such as the United States has never imagined; thousands of people will be involved.

We will see many new advances in science, as medical research begins to delve more deeply into the basis of life. This is cosmic action, or quasar energy activating the filament of each human cell. Medical science will discover how to bring these cells back to their normal vibrations so they will again be in balance with the cells around them. This breakthrough obviously will be important in cancer research and will also increase the span of life.

The Russians will complete the eighty SS-10 and SS-13 sites they are presently building. These will be sites from which they can launch an MIRV with multiple warheads, or an FOBS, for pinpoint observation and firing.

Also, we will see more phasing out of the Vietnam war and some economic recovery in the United States.

Nineteen seventy-five will be a year of internal upheaval in this country. Much rioting and accompanying sabotage will be covertly directed by our opposing forces. They will feel strong enough to move in Southeast Asia, South America, and Africa.

Nineteen seventy-six will see a drastic change in the government of the United States. This government will be committed to partial disarmament and appeasement.

In 1977 the Soviet Union will move openly and boldly to consolidate its position on three continents.

In 1978 the United States will be caught in the throes of a depression brought about by vast social and political giveaways and internal subversion.

Nineteen seventy-nine will see Russia turning its full attention to the Middle East. Israel will continue to be attacked by its neighbors.

In 1980 the world will experience a catastrophic earthquake.

Before going on to long-range prophecies, I want to make the basis for such prophecies clearly understood. It is this: no prophecy is absolute in its effect. This is why I give warnings, since changes for the better can be brought about by action, prayer, or invention. Every prediction is based on the conditions to which it is applied; a change in these conditions can and does affect the result. A "revelation," on the other hand, is not dependent upon conditions or circumstances; it is an absolute assurance of some future event, and only the timing is variable.

Catastrophe, therefore, as we read in the Book of Jonah, can always be averted or at least postponed by prayer and penance. But events such as the Second Coming of Jesus are revelations and are not subject to change. Only their timing is relative, as the birth of Jesus in the reign of Caesar Augustus, or the Second Coming as God's answer to the reign of the Antichrist. A "revelation" is a drawing aside of the veil of the future, as set forth in the Book of Revelation of Saint John. God shows through symbols and figures what is going to happen as a result of the free choices of men. The timing God has reserved to Himself, but the events are certain! Human freedom is not impaired by a revelation; God is simply showing what will happen as a result of a choice or series of choices, good or bad. In other words, God's revelation of an event does not determine the event itself; God is simply saying that a particular consequence will follow a specified course of action. In this sense God is simply the context of reality in which man lives.

The story of Jonah and Nineveh illustrates perfectly this mystery of freedom and foresight, and how they interact through God's justice and mercy.

Jonah was inspired by God to preach repentance in the great city of Nineveh, and knowing the hazards and responsibilities of prophecy, he declined. But God refused to take no for an answer, and in due course Jonah was walking the streets of Nineveh, crying: "Forty days more and Nineveh shall be destroyed!"

But "... the people of Nineveh believed God; they proclaimed a fast and all of them, great and small, put on sackcloth.

"When the news reached the king of Nineveh, he rose from his throne, laid aside his robe, covered himself with sackcloth, and sat in the ashes. Then he had this proclaimed throughout Nineveh, by decree of the king and his nobles: 'Neither man nor beast, neither cattle nor sheep, shall taste anything; they shall not eat, nor shall they drink water. Man and beast shall be covered with sackcloth and call loudly to God; every man shall turn from his evil way and from the violence he has in hand. Who knows, God may relent and forgive, and withhold his blazing wrath, so that we shall not perish.' When God saw by their actions how they turned from their evil way, he repented of the evil that he had threatened to do to them; he did not carry it out." (Jonah 3:4-10.)

Jonah did not know of God's reprieve until the forty days were past. He took up a position near the city, and when he saw that nothing happened, he could not bear the loss of face; he wanted to die.

Unlike Jonah, I hope that changes can be wrought in some of the following long-range prophecies; but I see no great disposition on the part of modern man to turn to God as the Ninevites did. How saving if they would!

On the contrary, it is impossible to pick up a newspaper, book, or magazine, or to see a movie, play, or television show, without being assaulted by the rising tide of religious or moral decadence assailing the human spirit everywhere. It is almost as if the awesome drama of *Faust* were being reenacted on a cosmic human scale!

This, of course, is not new. It has a long history. What is new is the success of the destructive element in human nature, which is now beginning to reverse totally on the past and attack history itself. By plan of the Communist countries, we are now being programmed to become a race of mindless people, happy but unknowing, with no sense of past or future, to live in a controlled present beyond freedom and dignity. We will be left with only our senses and feelings to guide us from a painless awakening in adolescence to a meaningless passage toward the rainbow oblivion of prolonged childhood.

The future has been shown to me to 2037. This

vision began in 1961 and is divided into nineteen-year cycles to 2020; then comes a seventeen-year period, ending in 2037. At the same time it must be borne in mind that such visions are like looking at an approaching landscape through the window of a vehicle or airplane: the closer the objects, the more clearly they are seen, whereas the relative perspective of the more distant components is less distinct. This is why biblical prophecy is so definite as to time and place of events to transpire in its own era, but in speaking of our times and beyond—the distant future—terminology is not as precise.

I have seen the number 19 over the President's foreign policy adviser. At first I did not know what this meant; but later the vision became clear to me that during the period 1961–1980, while our opponents grow stronger, we will live under a false sense of security brought about by our constant resort to compromise and negotiation. Then in 1980 we will begin to reap the harvest of our mistakes as greater trouble begins.

This period will be triggered by a natural disaster in the Middle East. An earthquake of major proportions will be the signal advantage for an invasion of Israel by its neighbors. Battles will continue until 1988, when the force of both sides will be greatly weakened. Then the Russians and their satellite armies will move into the area and occupy the lands of all participants. More battles, bloodshed, massacres, misery, and pestilence will continue until 1995; a time of turmoil and uneasy peace will last until about 1999.

During this time a phenomenon will take place which recalls the stand of Moses at the Red Sea in Israel's early history and the epochal deliverance of the Jews from the destructive armies of the ancient Egyptian Pharaoh. The Russians, like the Egyptians, will find that the intervention of God is irresistible and infinitely superior to the power of nations, armies, missiles, and human ingenuity.

Like the Jews in the time of Moses, Israel will fear the worst from its enemies—complete annihilation. All opposition and virtually all religion will have already been wiped out in the Middle East by the conquering armies. There will be almost no hope. The United States will find itself too weakened both economically and militarily to fight a major war. We will align ourselves with those powers who have most to lose by Communist domination of the world: England, France, Japan, Italy, Canada, Belgium, Germany, the Netherlands, and Sweden.

Since the major events will be in the Middle East, our headquarters will be in Rome. In 1995 great allied armies will begin the buildup to strike at the Russian forces, apprehensive despite all their success. They, of course, will place all the blame on the United States for what they will call aggressive moves against them; but our allies will not compromise because the leader in Rome will be in full control.

The Russians will then ready their MIRVs and FOBSs. As the armies begin to move on the Middle East about 1999, Russian MIRVs and FOBSs will rain down a nuclear holocaust upon our coastal cities, both east and west. From missile bases already established in the Carpathians will rain the same fire storms upon the cities of Europe. We will retaliate. There will be fear for the survival of all mankind ... and not without reason.

Into this maelstrom of destruction and confusion will come the intervention of God to save Israel and restore peace. "There will be signs in the sun, the moon and the stars." (Luke 21:25.)

"Immediately after the stress of that period, 'the sun will be darkened, the moon will not shed her light ... the hosts of heaven will be shaken.' Then the sign of the Son of Man will appear in the sky . . ." (Matthew 24:29-30.)

In the midst of all this, the greatest of shock waves will hit the earth, causing three days and three nights of darkness. "The stars and constellations of the heavens send forth no light; the sun is dark when it rises, and the light of the moon does not shine.... I will make the heavens tremble and the earth shall be shaken from its place...." (Isaiah 13:10-13.)

"... I will cover the heavens, and all their stars I will darken; the sun I will cover with clouds, and the moon shall not give its light. All the shining lights in the heavens I will darken on your account, and I will spread darkness over your land, says the Lord God." (Ezekiel 32:7-8.)

It is then that "the sign of the Son of Man will appear in the sky," that is, the Sign of the Cross in the sky, as it was seen in the days of Constantine, with the revelation: "In this sign thou shalt conquer."

There will be a striking historical similarity between the Roman armies of old at the Milvian Bridge and those at the end of the twentieth century moving on the Middle East. Both determine the history of the West for the next millennium: Constantine in establishing the religion which was to be the basis of all following Western culture, and the new Roman leader who will finally crush the Communist armies and clear the way for the new Judeo-Christian religion that is to be the spiritual faith of the new era beginning about the first half of the next century.

Later, when this flaming Sign of the Cross lights the desolate, darkened sky over the Great Rift Valley, God sends further consolation to Israel. Jesus is seen bodily in the Holy Land on the field of Armageddon. The Jews, hopelessly outnumbered and near the end of all hope, are galvanized by a resurgence of faith, unfelt since the times of the Maccabees. Understanding the miraculous intervention paralleling that of Moses and the Red Sea passage, they proclaim Jesus Christ as the true Messiah, crying out: "The Lord is my God! The Lord is our God!"

Meanwhile the divine intervention has also reached the battlefields. By the year 2000, the Communist armies in the Middle East will be completely isolated, with no home base of supply. They will be speedily destroyed by the armies led from Rome. Nuclear weapons from the sea and air will join those from ground forces in a rain of death on the trapped Communist armies. Unbearable heat will burn their bodies; the force of the blast and shock waves will tumble their tanks and equipment like toys. The intense flashes of nuclear lightning will blind thousands, who will wander aimlessly in the desert, only to die from wounds, burns, and the blazing heat of the sun. The leader in Rome will be hailed as a savior, ruler, and great, conquering hero.

What an ironic surprise he will be holding in store!

This phase will end quickly about the year 2005. Then the other Communist monster will begin to stir. Both the United States and Soviet Russia will have ceased to be great powers. China will be reaching the peak of its industrialization and will begin to move seriously toward world domination. Another series of battles will begin, to last for nineteen years. They will culminate about the year 2020 in the apocalyptic battle of Armageddon.

Read Chapter Sixteen of the Book of Revelation, which can refer to the modern nations and weapons of war in some of its symbols and metaphors. What I am relating is really a magnified version of part of the same vision—brought closer by two thousand years.

The Chinese armies will take all of Asia quickly, then gathering their hordes numbering in the hundreds of thousands, they will move like locusts overland toward the allied armies in the Middle East. Their leaders feel that their numbers alone, spread over thousands of miles, will be too many for even nuclear weapons to annihilate. They surmise enough of their armies will survive the blasts, radiation, and fire storms to defeat the armies of allied Rome. Great human waves pouring over each succeeding wave will be their strategy, and this will not change. Their numbers alone moving overland will pollute the earth. The carcasses of their dead millions, burned and blasted with heat and radiation from the allied missiles will increase the pollution, and resulting pestilence will kill more than the nuclear bombs and warheads. Those that arrive at the scene of battle will be so weakened that the armies of Rome will slaughter them by the millions.

At last the tide of battle turns, as all Europe unites against the common enemy, and the Roman leader is hailed as a savior, messiah, and God. He is in reality the Antichrist, or "beast," in the symbolism of Saint John, and is now in full command of the world. This is the "abominable and destructive thing which the prophet Daniel foretold standing on holy ground"—another translation says, "standing where it ought not"—"let the reader take note!" (Matthew 24:15.)

As I have indicated, in 2020 we have now reached the time focused on by Saint Matthew, Daniel, Isaiah, Micah and, again, Saint John. The Gospel of Saint Matthew continues: "... those in Judea must flee to the mountains. If a man is on the roof terrace, he must not come down to get anything out of his house. If a man is in the field, he must not turn back to pick up his cloak. It will be hard on pregnant or nursing mothers in those days. Keep praying that you will not have to flee in winter or on a sabbath, for those days will be more filled with anguish than any from the beginning of the world until now or in all ages to come. Indeed, if the period had not been shortened, not a human being would be saved. For the sake of the chosen, however, the days will be shortened.

"If anyone tells you at that time, 'Look, the Messiah is

here,' or 'He is there,' do not believe it. False messiahs and false prophets will appear, performing signs and wonders so great as to mislead even the chosen if that were possible. Remember, I have told you all about it beforehand. . . . As the lightning from the east flashes to the west, so will the coming of the Son of Man be." (Matthew 24:16-27.)

Deliverance from the reign of the Antichrist can come only from the continuing intervention of God. His power is so great that "It forced all men, small and great, rich and poor, slave and free, to accept a stamped image on their right hand or their forehead. Moreover, it did not allow a man to buy or sell anything unless he was first marked with the name of the beast or with the number that stood for its name." (Revelation 13:16-17.)

The Antichrist, now in full command of the world, is the "abominable and destructive thing"—or the "abomination of desolation"—spoken of by Daniel the prophet, standing in the holy place. Like Daniel, I see the vision become indistinct after that, as the dreaded number 19 changes to 17, indicating the beginning of the new seventeen-year cycle. The year is approximately 2020, and in the years immediately following the Antichrist disappears. The years 2020–2037, approximately, hail the true Second Coming of Christ. His people, the surviving Jews, are spreading the Gospel throughout the world. Their persecution has ended with the passing of the worst religious persecution ever known, and they have become the key to a new Judeo-Christian faith of the new era. I see this as an era of light, glory, and unprecedented human happiness and goodwill beyond the year 2037, all under the auspices of the renewed spirit of Jesus in the world. His plan for the future of man, under His guidance, will begin to unfold, and our acceptance will grow with our understanding that one world under God can flourish despite—and because of—differences of religious denomination. We will be in the days spoken of by Isaiah, in a prophecy now carved in part on a wall at the United Nations in New York, when there will be peace in the world and all men shall go up to the temple of the Lord to seek the salvation of God.

Instead of the dirty, blighted cities of the past, I see in this new world great bright, shining centers of religion, learning, commerce, and art. Industry and transportation will flourish as man learns to live in harmony with his environment and his spiritual heritage. Education once again will acquaint the man and woman of the future with the idea of what a noble thing it is to be a human being, and awaken to the privilege of developing and using our divinely granted talents in the great enterprise of man and God. The lessons, terrifying and unforgettable, of the immediate past will reinforce these concepts as men and women perceive how necessary and good it is to live in peace with other men and women throughout the world and in balance with the thousands of species of animals, birds, insects, fish, and vegetative life in nature. Waste will be used to fertilize, build, and recycle. Problems of ecology will disappear as science makes pollution and waste obsolete terms.

The world's population will increase slowly again, after the horrendous and devastating experience of Armageddon. The Malthusian problem will not recur. The discovery of marvelous new metals, materials, and sources of energy, atomic, cosmic, and magnetic, will not only revolutionize life and industry, but will make it possible to engage in space travel of distances that are inconceivable now, at close to the speed of light. Advances in medical knowledge will bring cancer, heart disease, and even the common cold under control! The secrets of the nervous system will begin to unfold. Surgery of the future will be performed by an electrochemical process. The basic knowledge of the source of life, the core of the human cell energized by cosmic action, will make possible the transplanting of organs and even the formation of new organs and members. The ordinary life-span will become much longer. Marvels of the human brain will be understood. Cybernetics will be developed in ways that would now baffle the mind and stagger the imagination. A loosely knit form of democratic world government will oversee world problems, while each sovereign state will maintain its identity, much as American states do, or as countries which were members of the British Commonwealth of Nations. This new commonwealth of states will be world-wide, a truly United Nations! Regulation of trade will be nominal, purposeful, and limited. The life of the individual within society will be much more human, dignified, responsible, and free than any known standards of the past.

As the new era picks up momentum during the 2030's, the new spiritual reign of Jesus will turn the world into a near paradise which will sow the seeds of life on this new human level throughout the universe. This is the great mission of man. This is what Jesus envisioned for us, created by God in His image and likeness, with intelligence and free will. This is the full understanding of His declaration: "I came that they might have life and have it to the full." (John 10:10.)

This is our destiny.

By the next mid-century mark, the Second Coming of Christ, the lifting of the veil over the secrets of life, the opening up of the universe to discovery and colonization by man—this is the future I see. It is incomplete and puzzling in some ways, but the more I pray and meditate upon it, the more I understand.

Man will look back on the years of Armageddon and realize how close he came to total destruction. He will read the life and times of the twentieth century with incredulity and wonder, much as Europeans read the history of America during the Gilded Age. He will understand at last the depth of meaning in the words of Jesus, "I am the way, and the truth, and the life." He will comprehend his own transfiguration in Jesus and grasp the meaning of his share in the words of God as they apply to all of us: "This is my beloved son. My favor rests on him."

He will understand the meaning of the words I have learned from the Jesus of the Gospel and the Resurrection: "Seek life in me, for in my name there is no beginning, nor is there any end."

"The night shall be no more. They will need no light from lamps or the sun, for the Lord God shall give them light, and they shall reign forever." (Revelation 22:5.)

I see the end and the beginning—a new era, a new life, a new world.

—Jeane Dixon

Epilogue

Like most people I am trying to live a useful life. I have tried to follow as closely as possible His divine guidance, to fulfill my mission and purpose in accordance with His plan for me. In doing so, I have had many disappointments, and usually in those I have loved and helped the most. I have experienced real sorrow; but then, too, joy, happiness, and much love have also been mine. The suffering and troubles that came my way were peculiarly my own. As time goes by, I comprehend a deeper sense of things as a whole. But then, we were not told that life would be easy, were we? So I try to view things as they fit for me into God's plan for my life.

I feel the abiding presence of the Lord Jesus as He wept over Jerusalem, because, as He said, He could see the results of His people's refusal to accept the time of divine visitation. I see us making the same tragic mistake today with the same woeful consequences. When Jesus spoke of the calamities soon to come upon His people, the Pharisees demanded a sign and He refused it, except the sign of His own death and resurrection (Matthew 12:38-40), demanding that they read instead the signs of the times. They chose instead to destroy Him; and the calamities came. I feel my own small gift to my own era is also being ignored. I trust not, lest calamities result.

Our world is a much greater and wider one than the little community over which Jesus wept that night in Jerusalem. He did His work perfectly! His religion spread out from there around the world and back!

As I ponder upon this world after so many years of following Him, I find many things move me to tears. One thing that invariably does is the vision of our whole earth in perspective, the view in part photographed by our astronauts in space.

There it is! In all its beauty and splendor! Why does it make me weep? A little ball of green, tufted earth, air, clouds, and water, floating serenely in the void of space, acting out its brief ballet of phenomena and history to the deep, tranquil music of the spheres. It seems such a little, fragile thing, like a newborn baby; yet at the same time, it also seems like a great cosmic miracle carrying the divine gift of life.

How many floating islands are there like it in the illimitable ocean of space? It is too soon to know that yet, just as it was too soon for Jesus to speak about us and our part in His mission the night He wept over Jerusalem. Still, I can feel that Divine, brooding Presence, as if Jesus were weeping now over our modern world for the same reasons: division, destruction, death, and desolation, "... because you failed to recognize the time of your visitation." (Luke 19:44.)

As the earthly journey of Jesus of Nazareth neared its end, not only Peter and the apostles but the crowds who followed Him and the Roman centurion in charge of the Crucifixion on Calvary believed that for a fleeting moment man had been privileged to look into the face of God. "Clearly this man was the Son of God," said the centurion. As the darkness of that first Good Friday deepened and then lifted, first a woman and then a few men, still lingering on Golgotha Hill, realized that His presence had not been irrevocably lost to the human spirit. All the goodness and beauty of man's soul, as Jesus taught it, could be the heritage of each coming age. "Go, therefore, and make disciples of all the nations." (Matthew 28:19.) It was actually God's plan to take Israel to the world.

This has been the message of this book. I have tried to pass on what is so clear to me. I realized how strange it may sound at first to the layman and the critic! But the simplest truths are often the hardest to accept. What would you have said if you had been living in 1492 and read that an adventurer named Columbus, believing that the world was round, had sailed off to discover a new world—or at least a new route to India? What was to happen in the next five centuries was beyond all imagination. What would you have said to the Wright Brothers if they had told you at Kitty Hawk that within a century more people would be flying across oceans and continents in their newfangled machine than sailing in the greatest ships? What would you have said in 1918, after the "war to end all wars," if someone had whispered in your ear that in two short decades we would have to go through the whole thing all over again? The truth of things is often impossible for us to accept—until it comes to pass!

I am saying that religion is nothing if not startling. I have been saying that when Abraham, the patriarch, went down from Mesopotamia to Palestine nearly four thousand years ago he began a journey that was even more significant than the voyage of Columbus a few millennia later or our first flight to the moon. It was a short trip for Abraham but one that would never end for mankind!

I have been saying in this book that Abraham and Moses built the world of the prophets and that the prophets prepared the way for Israel to reach out with a message from God for all humanity. It reached the world through Christianity and the civilization that Christianity spread through the world during the almost two thousand years when Israel was not a nation. I realize that I have been saying startling things, just as the ancient prophets did, and just as true. I have referred to the resurrection of Israel in 1948 as the beginning of a spiritual revival for Israel in the light of the Resurrection of Jesus and linking the two. I have said that the vision of the Transfiguration applies to all religion in a transfigured world of the future, where the new Jerusalem will be the spiritual capital of the world in a new age. I have said that this age could evolve peacefully, but that it is more likely that the end of our era will come with unprecedented suffering and war.

I realize full well the meaning of my words. It has not been easy for me to say some of these things: I love my fellow men and women as much as anyone and I wish them all well. I feel the grave obligation to use my gift of prophecy and wish to use it well and fully.

Jesus of Nazareth, a Galilean rabbi, whose life marked the watershed of human history, is the key figure of Isaiah's message, as He is the goal of Isaiah's Messianic prophecy. Baruch Spinoza, a Portuguese Jew, called Him ". . . The unrealized ideal of humanity." Only He is capable of getting us all together: Buddhists from the East, Hindus from India and Ceylon, Mohammedans from Africa and western Asia, people of all the residual faiths of China and Japan, pagans from Europe and America, Marxists from everywhere. Unity cannot be achieved by science, government, or abstract ideas; what we need is a Messiah! God has already given us one.

The Ecumenical Movement is far advanced. Even Jews and Christians are coming together in long overdue brotherhood. We are beginning to notice that the Mass or Eucharist is really a celebration of the Last Supper, which is really the celebration of the Passover, with Jesus in the place of honor! A rabbi speaks of a "Jewish

Easter." Christians used to speak of the "conversion of
the Jews"; but now a Jewish rabbi speaks of the
"Judaization of Christianity." They mean the same
thing. Jesus was the loyal dissenter who fell victim to
conspiratorial and formal bureaucracy. His heavenly Father was the God of the Jews: "He who gives me glory is
the Father, the very one you claim for your God." (John
8:54.) He went on to say that we all share in that
divinity as in our common humanity: "Is it not written
in your law, 'I have said, You are gods'?" (John 10:34.)

A unifying religion is the true hope of the world for
the reign of peace and love. This, indeed, is what is
meant by the expression "The reign of God."

I believe that the rise of the state of Israel, like that
of early Christianity, is the answer of a loving God to
provide man with the opportunity for a new era. I see
the providential role of Jews all over the world, especially in America assuring Israel of the existence and greatness God promised to Abraham and Moses for its mission to the world. This mission is the most ancient and
the most modern. It is entering upon a new spiritual
renaissance.

*I see a great historic future for Israel, a future that is
worthy of the best of her long history, tradition, and
destiny. I see that the "new Jerusalem" to come is the
key to the world's religious fulfillment as Rome was the
key to humanity's survival in the Dark Ages. I see the
new Israel, "the mountain of the House of the Lord," as
the key to the most glorious age that man has ever
known. . . . And it lies just beyond the worst age . . . that
lies ahead before the end of our present dark age.*

What of the Resurrection and Christ's Second Coming?

Nothing in Christianity has excited people more than
the "Second Coming." This event has been awaited with
the same rising expectation built up after Isaiah's proclamation of His first advent.

Theologians now accept a more spiritual interpretation of the Second Coming of Christ than the believers of other times. However, according to the thinking of Christian theologians of all times, it will be universal; as the figure of the lightning from the east that "flashes to the west, so will the coming of the Son of Man be." (Matthew 24:27.) Yet it is constant and ongoing at all times, as Jesus said to people listening to Him before His death. "I assure you, among those standing here there are some who will not experience death before they see the Son of Man come in his kingship." (Matthew 16:28.) Another time He told His apostles, "When they persecute you in one town, flee to the next. I solemnly assure you, you will not have covered the towns of Israel before the Son of Man comes." (Matthew 10:23.) When pressed on this point by the Pharisees, who asked the definite question, when the kingdom of God would come, Jesus replied: "You cannot tell by careful watching when the reign of God will come. Neither is it a matter of reporting that it is 'here' or 'there.' The reign of God is already in your midst." (Luke 17:20-21.) Hence the conviction has grown that the Second Coming began with the Resurrection and will reach a dynamic, historic climax at some future time.

I have been saying that we are living in the age of the Resurrection and the Second Coming. Although we are not always aware of it, the reign of God is already in our midst; yet it is a great historic and universal event as well. The Messiah, having once come, now tarries through the long night of history like the householder in the Gospel banquet. But the night is far spent, and we must live in expectation of the Master's return.

The greatest events in religious history are still ahead! The idea of the main and central event is not new: the coming of Jesus in spirit and in truth through the regeneration of individuals and the unification of all religious bodies. The Messiah comes for all men if He comes at all. His Second Coming will indeed be in "great power and majesty" as the Gospel proclaims, but it will likewise be under the Sign of the Cross. He left as a Jew and will return as a Jew to be acclaimed by His own people as well as all others.

"All mankind shall see the salvation of God." (Luke 3:6.) Isaiah describes for me the condition of the new world society to come in words often quoted at Christmas, as the lion lies down with the lamb and the leopard is the guest of the kid: "There shall be no harm or ruin on all my holy mountain; for the earth shall be filled with knowledge of the Lord, as the water covers the sea." (Isaiah 11:9.) At last man will understand!

I have written about the "Sign of the Cross" at some length in the preceding chapter. These words stand for the days spoken of by Jesus preceding His Second Coming. It is likewise symbolic of the deep human suffering I see in our future before the full return of Jesus to Israel and Israel to the world.

We have seen the death and desolation of so many caught by circumstances between the Nazis and the Communists. Many escaped the bondage of the one only to become the captives of the other. The Jews have been the worst sufferers, but the calamities of our century have left none of us unscarred. The present is bleak; the future looms worse. Because of our lack of understanding, people live for false values rather than the true religious values. The worst of all our false standards is a blind materialism—unless we learn to control it, all will fail!

There is only one true path for all humanity and that is the path of Jesus. Like others before me, I know this; I can see through to a better world beyond, a world that still will be forced by divine intervention to lay down its arms and devote its energies to prayer, peace, and justice—which is God's plan for all the world even now!

In a recent vision I saw this embodied symbolically in

the act of Pontius Pilate washing his hands of the condemnation of Jesus.

A vision appeared—and in this vision I was standing alone in the desert. I looked to my left, and there was a prison. In the vision I knew without being told that Barabbas was imprisoned there; he was not one of the robbers crucified on a cross beside Jesus, but a thief and a murderer.

Then, looking straight ahead, I saw Pontius Pilate sitting on a chair that was elevated. It was not a throne, but a very important-looking chair, a chair to be used only by one in authority.

I turned my gaze to the right, where hills rose from the plain, and saw someone walking very slowly down the hillside toward us. At the foot of the hill He stopped on a grassy knoll and looked out over the desert. I saw the grass had turned brown beneath His feet as He stood, and I knew that this was Jesus.

Again, I turned to the left; somehow a huge crowd of people had assembled where at first there had been only the prison.

Wondering, I looked again at Pontius Pilate sitting in the elevated chair. He was saying: "You shall make the decision . . . you shall make the decision."

The crowd shouted back as with one voice: "Free Barabbas! Free Barabbas! Persecute Jesus! Persecute Jesus!"

Replying, Pontius Pilate again twice repeated his words: "You have made the decision . . . you have made the decision. Free Barabbas . . . free Barabbas!"

But he did not say, "Persecute Jesus!"

Sadly, I turned to my left. I saw Barabbas freed from the prison, whereupon he led the people to the left between the prison and the chair of Pontius Pilate. He continued to lead the people, and in my vision they trampled over other people, over buildings, over heads of state, over government structures, and everything in their pathway was left in utter shambles.

At last I saw a lighted steeple, a small steeple pointing heavenward, atop a church. It seemed like a beacon in the darkness—but it was also destroyed by the mob.

Once more I heard the voice of Pontius Pilate. "When the evil of one man can lead the masses to destruction, then no longer can the majority rule the earth or the Church!"

Loudly he repeated it: "When the evil of one man can lead the masses to destruction, then no longer can the majority rule the earth or the Church!"

Silence descended on the desert—a silence so loud you could hear its stillness. In that awful, ominous silence came another voice from above me, from in back of me, from in front, from all around, it came pleading:

"FOLLOW ME!

"FOLLOW ME!

"FOLLOW ME!"

It was the voice of Jesus.